To CLAUDIA,

[signature]

PSA 111-3

FIRE STARTERS

Daily Conversations with God

RON VIETTI

Copyright © 2019 by Ron Vietti

Scripture quotations are from the ESV® Bible (The Holy Bible, English Standard Version®), copyright © 2001 by Crossway, a publishing ministry of Good News Publishers. Used by permission. All rights reserved.

Scripture quotations marked (NLT) are taken from the Holy Bible, New Living Translation, copyright ©1996, 2004, 2015 by Tyndale House Foundation. Used by permission of Tyndale House Publishers, Inc., Carol Stream, Illinois 60188. All rights reserved.

Scripture quotations marked (NIV) are taken from the Holy Bible, New International Version®, NIV®. Copyright © 1973, 1978, 1984, 2011 by Biblica, Inc.™ Used by permission of Zondervan. All rights reserved worldwide. www.zondervan.com The "NIV" and "New International Version" are trademarks registered in the United States Patent and Trademark Office by Biblica, Inc.™

Scripture quotations taken from the New American Standard Bible® (NASB), Copyright © 1960, 1962, 1963, 1968, 1971, 1972, 1973, 1975, 1977, 1995 by The Lockman Foundation. Used by permission. www.Lockman.org All rights reserved.

Scripture taken from the New King James Version®. Copyright © 1982 by Thomas Nelson. Used by permission. All rights reserved.

No part of this book may be reproduced in any form without permission in writing from the publisher, except in the case of brief quotations embodied in articles or reviews.

Published by Ron Vietti
ISBN: 978-0-9982996-3-1
Printed in the United States of America

ACKNOWLEDGMENTS

I want to say a special thanks to Nicole Dickey. Without you I couldn't do a lot of things.

To my daughter Tara who I simply think is the greatest daughter in the whole world, and the one whose insight I could not do without.

(Without you two, this book never would have made it to the printer.)

To my wife Debbie, for 50 years of staying married to a guy who has tested her patience in every way possible, without you I don't know where I would be.

A special thanks to my son Josh for the title and cover. He is the creative one in the family, and the best son a dad could ever want.

To my grandkids, Kylee, Kenzee, and Josiah. You guys are the real deal. And to my little princess Olive and my granddaughter soon-to-be here. I love you all dearly.

To the best daughter-in-law and son-in-law in the world, Ashley and Jim. I am truly blessed.

INTRODUCTION

This book was written for people who have a relationship with God. It is meant to be used as an example of things we can pray about daily. The prayers are not meant to be repeated word for word, but to be expressed in your own words to God.

I hope this book will give new believers in Christ an introduction on how to pray.

When we pray as believers, we pray in Jesus' name. That doesn't mean that we use His name as a magic formula at the end of a prayer. It just simply means that we recognize that it is through Jesus that we have access to God the Father, and we are praying according to what we believe to be His will. Some people prefer to add that to the end of their prayers as a reminder, and that is quite okay.

It is my hope that this book will help us learn how to pray and talk to God in a very personal way. It is also my hope that we will become more acquainted with His will for our life as we pray according to Scripture.

DAY 1
Abandonment

"Lord, let me know that I am never alone. You said in Your Word that You would never leave me nor forsake me. Thank You for being with me today. Let me feel Your presence. Amen."

For my father and my mother have forsaken me, but the Lord will take me in.
Psalm 27:10 ESV

DAY 2
Absentminded

"*Lord*, today I need Your help in remembering what is important and what is not important. Please remind me to do the things that I need to do. Without Your help I know I will forget. Amen."

But the Helper, the Holy Spirit, whom the Father will send in My name, He will teach you all things, and bring to remembrance all that I said to you.
John 14:26 NASB

DAY 3
Acceptance

"*Lord*, please help me to realize that not everyone is going to accept me. Help me to be loved and accepted by the people that You want in my life, and help me not to worry about the others. Cause the need for acceptance to never be something that defines me. Help me to be more concerned about accepting others than being accepted. Amen."

For God does not show favoritism.
Romans 2:11 NLT

DAY 4
Accomplishment

"Lord, today help me to see how easy it is to accomplish Your will. Every little loving deed I do for others will be noticed by You. Help me to live with others in mind. Help me to pray for others, encourage others, give to others, and help others. Let me see that no little thing done for another person is too small to be pleasing in Your sight. Amen."

For it is God's will that by doing good you should silence the ignorant talk of foolish people.
1 Peter 2:15 NIV

DAY 5
Accusations

"Lord, today I refuse to worry about people who accuse me of wrongdoing. If their accusation is true, I will apologize and right the wrong if I can. If it's not true, I will ask You to defend me and take up my cause. Either way, I will win in the end. Amen."

Having a good conscience, so that, when you are slandered, those who revile your good behavior in Christ may be put to shame.
1 Peter 3:16 ESV

DAY 6
Addiction

"*Lord*, please help me to overcome all addictions in my life. I know it's not Your will for me to be in slavery to drugs, alcohol, food, relationships, money, or any other thing in life. With Your help I can enjoy all good things without being addicted. I need Your continual help to keep me free from the bondage of all things that seek to control my life. Amen."

"I have the right to do anything," you say - but not everything is beneficial. "I have the right to do anything" - but I will not be mastered by anything.
1 Corinthians 6:12 NIV

DAY 7
Advice

"*Lord*, help me not to be too proud to take advice from godly people. Teach me that in order to live the productive life You have called me to, occasionally I will have to seek out counsel and wisdom from others. Amen."

Without wise leadership, a nation falls; there is safety in having many advisers.
Proverbs 11:14 NLT

DAY 8
Affirmation

"*Lord*, we know that everyone needs some amount of affirmation. Today please give me some affirming words to take into the world. Cause me to have the right words to affirm everyone I see. Give me the ability to look at other's strengths and talents, and be able to encourage them with the gifts that You have given them. Amen."

So encourage each other and build each other up, just as you are already doing.
1 Thessalonians 5:11 NLT

DAY 9
Ambition

"*Lord*, I have a tendency to get lazy. Please awaken my spirit today, and make me ambitious about Your will and purpose for my life. Birth new desires and rekindle old desires in my heart. Please help me to accomplish some great things for You in my lifetime starting today. Amen."

Call to Me and I will answer you, and I will tell you great and mighty things, which you do not know.
Jeremiah 33:3 NASB

DAY 10
Angels

"Lord, give your angels charge concerning me and my family today. Don't let us go anywhere without Your holy angels watching over us. If any evil tries to overcome us, cause Your angels to be there to help us and protect us. Amen."

For He will give His angels charge concerning you, to guard you in all your ways.
Psalm 91:11 NASB

DAY 11

Anger

"Lord, today help me to take the things that make me angry and rechannel them in a productive way. Cause me to see that the anger of man does not have the capability to accomplish God's will unless it is channeled in a constructive way. Help me to be creative in my angry moments. Amen."

*Human anger does not produce
the righteousness God desires.
James 1:20 NLT*

DAY 12

Answers

"Lord, I need Your help to recognize Your answers to my prayers when they come. So often because of my preconceived notions about how I think You should answer, I miss the real answer when it comes. Also, help me to realize that sometimes when You don't answer my prayer, that is an answer to my prayer. Help me to accept a no as well as a yes. Amen."

Therefore I tell you, whatever you ask in prayer, believe that you have received it, and it will be yours.
Mark 11:24 ESV

DAY 13
Apology

"Lord, I know that I sometimes offend people, and I say and do things that hurt others. Please give me the courage and strength to never be ashamed to apologize whenever it becomes apparent that I have done wrong, and give me the resolve to always accept the apology of another. Amen."

Be kind to one another, tenderhearted, forgiving one another, as God in Christ forgave you.
Ephesians 4:32 ESV

DAY 14
Appreciation

"Lord, thank You for all the wonderful people You have surrounded me with. Help me to never take them for granted. Give me the opportunity to show them how much they mean to me on a regular basis. They may not always be here. Amen."

Every time I think of you, I give thanks to my God.
Philippians 1:3 NLT

DAY 15
Arrogance

"*Lord*, help me to never think more highly of myself than I should. Please be gracious with me, but do whatever You need to do to keep me humble. Help me to see myself as You see me. Amen."

For by the grace given to me I say to everyone among you not to think of himself more highly than he ought to think, but to think with sober judgment, each according to the measure of faith that God has assigned.
Romans 12:3 ESV

DAY 16
Assumption

"*Lord*, give me the wisdom to never assume too many things, but to bring everything to You in prayer. Cause me to learn from the mistakes of many in the past who have suffered great defeat at the hands of assumption. Amen."

And all the people shall hear and fear and not act presumptuously again.
Deuteronomy 17:13 ESV

DAY 17
Assurance

"*Lord*, help me to see that every word You have spoken to mankind can be relied upon. Help us to never doubt the words that You have given to us. Let me rest assured that Your holy Word is more trustworthy than anything in life. Today cause me to live with confidence in Your Word. Amen."

But whoever keeps His word, in him the love of God has truly been perfected. By this we know that we are in Him.
1 John 2:5 NASB

DAY 18
Availability

"*Lord*, let us know that all You need in order to do great things on this earth is a person who is willing to let You live Your life through them. You can change the world through anyone who is available to be a conduit for Your great mercy and love. Today help me to be Your hands and feet in this world. Amen."

Then I heard the voice of the Lord, saying,
"Whom shall I send, and who will go for Us?"
Then I said, "Here am I. Send me!"
Isaiah 6:8 NASB

DAY 19
Awe

"*Lord*, cause me to see Your great glory in creation. As I see the heavens and the earth and the seas, cause me to realize that they are all the works of Your creative power. You are the creator of all things. Today cause me to stand in awe of Your greatness and glory. Amen."

Let all the earth fear the Lord; let all the inhabitants of the world stand in awe of Him.
Psalm 33:8 NASB

DAY 20
Backsliding

"*Lord*, I need Your help in order to keep growing. Help me to continually see the need for change. Once I stop changing I stop growing. You have called me to grow into the stature of Jesus, and I must never stop growing and changing as long as I am on this earth. Show me the areas where You want to change me today. Amen."

An intelligent heart acquires knowledge, and the ear of the wise seeks knowledge.
Proverbs 18:15 ESV

DAY 21
Balance

"*Lord*, help me to avoid extremes in every area of my life except in my love for You. Help me to acknowledge any areas of my life that are starting to get out of control. My love and commitment to You needs to remain my top priority in life; cause me to never let anything get in the way of that. Today keep me balanced in all areas of life. Amen."

Seek the Kingdom of God above all else, and live righteously, and he will give you everything you need.
Matthew 6:33 NLT

DAY 22
Bashful

"*Lord*, there are people out there in my world today who need to be touched with Your love. You have graciously given me talents and gifts that I need to use for Your glory. Help me not to let a bashful spirit get in the way of these things. Give me the strength and courage to be bold and to do what You have called me to do. Amen."

For God has not given us a spirit of timidity, but of power and love and discipline.
2 Timothy 1:7 NASB

DAY 23
Basics

"*Lord*, help me to never stop doing the basics. Daily I need to remain in Your Word and pray. Today I need to spend time in Your presence. Help me to make this a daily routine, and cause me to make any changes in my schedule that are necessary to make sure that these things remain a priority. Amen."

Abide in Me, and I in you. As the branch cannot bear fruit of itself unless it abides in the vine, so neither can you unless you abide in Me.
John 15:4 NASB

DAY 24
Beginning

"*Lord*, today is the beginning of the first day of the rest of my life. Help me to make the changes I need to make so that I will bear fruit in the years to come. Today cause me to stop procrastinating, and help me to begin to do the things You have called me to do. Beginning something is sometimes the hardest thing to do. Let today be the start of something new. Amen."

Arise, shine, for your light has come, and the glory of the Lord has risen upon you.
Isaiah 60:1 ESV

DAY 25
Behavior

"*Lord*, today let my behavior draw people to You. People may never read a Bible, but they will read my life. They will watch the things I do and they will hear the things I say, and all of those will have a reflection on You. Cause my life to be lived in such a way that it causes people to want to know more about You. Amen."

But the fruit of the Spirit is love, joy, peace, patience, kindness, goodness, faithfulness, gentleness, self-control; against such things there is no law.
Galatians 5:22-23 ESV

DAY 26
Bible

"*Lord*, help me to understand that the Bible is Your words given to mankind. Help me to understand the teachings of Your Word so I can have success in life. There is no source of truth on this earth that is greater than Your Word. Help me to cherish it, study it, defend it, and most of all, live by it. Amen."

All Scripture is God-breathed and is useful for teaching, rebuking, correcting and training in righteousness, so that the servant of God may be thoroughly equipped for every good work.
2 Timothy 3:16-17 NIV

DAY 27
Bitterness

"*Lord*, help me to never let a root of bitterness take hold in my life. Cause me to take every little thing that angers me to You in prayer, and don't let me stop praying until I find some sort of resolve. Give me the strength to forgive others and to not hold grudges in my life against anyone, knowing that these unresolved feelings can turn into a spirit of bitterness if retained. Bitterness will destroy my life, so help me today to forgive anyone who has hurt me. Amen."

See to it that no one fails to obtain the grace of God; that no "root of bitterness" springs up and causes trouble, and by it many become defiled.
Hebrews 12:15 ESV

DAY 28
Blame

"*Lord*, help me to take responsibility and own up to the areas of failure in my life. Help me to stop casting blame on others for what hasn't gone right in my life. Blaming others has no redemptive quality in it at all. So give me the courage today to let others go free from the blame that I have cast on them for the problems in my life. Amen."

The man said, "The woman you put here with me-she gave me some fruit from the tree, and I ate it."
Genesis 3:12 NIV

DAY 29
Blessing

"*Lord*, help me to recognize Your blessings in my life today. I know that You bless Your children, so help me to acknowledge all the areas of my life where you have blessed me. Let me understand that I have been blessed in order to be a blessing to others. Cause me to go out and bless others with some of the same blessings You have blessed me with. Amen."

Blessed be the God and Father of our Lord Jesus Christ, the Father of mercies and God of all comfort, who comforts us in all our affliction, so that we may be able to comfort those who are in any affliction with the comfort with which we ourselves are comforted by God.
2 Corinthians 1:3-4 ESV

DAY 30
Body

"*Lord*, help me to realize today that You gave me a body in order that I might be able to communicate Your love to the world. It is my earth suit. It is the temple of God. It is my responsibility to take care of this body and to keep it in good working order. Please help me to understand the things I need to do in order to keep it healthy. Amen."

Or do you not know that your body is a temple of the Holy Spirit within you, whom you have from God? You are not your own, for you were bought with a price. So glorify God in your body.
1 Corinthians 6:19-20 ESV

DAY 31
Brevity

"*Lord*, today help me not to belittle the idea of brevity. The Lord's Prayer that He taught His disciples was only 66 words long. Jesus modeled the idea of brevity for us in many ways. Cause me to see today that one verse read and understood is sometimes better than an hour-long Bible study. One heartfelt prayer prayed with faith and expectation can sometimes exceed the need for long prayers. Today help me to appreciate the power of brevity. Amen."

And when you are praying, do not use meaningless repetition as the Gentiles do, for they suppose that they will be heard for their many words.
Matthew 6:7 NASB

DAY 32
Burnout

"Lord, give me a spirit of discernment to recognize the things I may be doing that You have not called me to do. You will not call me to do so many things that it will cause me to burnout. Please show me anything I need to give up today. Amen."

But they who wait for the Lord shall renew their strength; they shall mount up with wings like eagles; they shall run and not be weary; they shall walk and not faint.
Isaiah 40:31 ESV

DAY 33
Caring

"*Lord*, help me to see the lack of real caring and unselfish love in this world we live in. Sometimes, just one little act of kindness can make a strong impression in someone's life. Today help me to know how to show concern and kindness to every person I meet. Amen."

Let each of you look not only to his own interests, but also to the interests of others.
Philippians 2:4 ESV

DAY 34
Carnality

"*Lord*, help me not to be a carnal Christian. Help me to live not only on the physical, material level but also on the spiritual level. Cause me to recognize that the spiritual world is as real as the physical and material world. Today help me to know when to stop talking and when to start praying. Also show me when to refrain from having to do things myself and when to turn things over to You. Amen."

But people who aren't spiritual can't receive these truths from God's Spirit. It all sounds foolish to them and they can't understand it, for only those who are spiritual can understand what the Spirit means.
1 Corinthians 2:14 NLT

DAY 35
Celebrate

"Lord, today give me a spirit of celebration. Cause me to see that a lot of things that happen in life are worthy of celebration. Cause me to not be embarrassed in celebrating the small, worthy accomplishments of those around me. Amen."

Also that everyone should eat and drink and take pleasure in all his toil - this is God's gift to man.
Ecclesiastes 3:13 ESV

DAY 36
Challenges

"*Lord*, cause me to see that without challenges in life my faith would not have the opportunity to grow. There will always be mountains that need to be climbed and rivers that need to be crossed in order to get to where God wants me to be. Today with the help of Your Spirit, don't let me be afraid to face the challenges of life head-on and see them as opportunities to grow. Amen."

Dear brothers and sisters, when troubles of any kind come your way, consider it an opportunity for great joy. For you know that when your faith is tested, your endurance has a chance to grow.
James 1:2-3 NLT

DAY 37

Change

"Lord, You have come into my life to change me. Don't let me be afraid of change. Today cause me to see the areas of my life that need to be transformed, and show me the baby steps necessary to start the process of change in those areas. Amen."

Therefore, if anyone is in Christ, he is a new creation. The old has passed away; behold, the new has come.
2 Corinthians 5:17 ESV

DAY 38
Character

"Lord, my character is who I am in the dark. Cause me to understand that You will never stop working on my character. Today I give You permission to allow whatever needs to come into my life in order to forge character in me. Help me to see that a good character is to be more desired than riches and fame. Amen."

A good name is to be chosen rather than great riches, and favor is better than silver or gold.
Proverbs 22:1 ESV

DAY 39
Charity

"*Lord*, help me to be willing to share with others some of what You have blessed me with. Deliver me from the quality of self-centeredness, and cause me to care more about those who are less fortunate in life. Amen."

Do not neglect to do good and to share what you have, for such sacrifices are pleasing to God.
Hebrews 13:16 ESV

DAY 40
Cheerful

"*Lord*, help me to have a cheerful spirit today. Let me show the people I meet the difference Christ makes in a life. Cause my mind to be focused on all the good things in my life instead of the bad things, so my cheerfulness will be authentic. Amen."

All the days of the afflicted are evil, but the cheerful of heart has a continual feast.
Proverbs 15:15 ESV

DAY 41
Choices

"Lord, today give me the wisdom and counsel I need to make wise decisions. Cause me to have faith in Your promise to give me wisdom if I wait on You. Cause my choices to reflect Your wisdom and be a testimony to Your faithfulness. Amen."

For the LORD gives wisdom; from His mouth come knowledge and understanding.
Proverbs 2:6 NASB

DAY 42
Commitment

"*Lord*, show me the things that are worthy of my commitment. Help me to have the foresight to not commit to too many things. Give me the wisdom to know that I only have so much energy and time, and I must be careful with what I commit to. Once I do make a commitment, give me the courage to see that commitment through to the end. Remind me that commitment helps grow my character. Amen."

If a man vows a vow to the Lord, or swears an oath to bind himself by a pledge, he shall not break his word. He shall do according to all that proceeds out of his mouth.
Numbers 30:2 ESV

DAY 43
Communication

"*Lord*, cause me to always say enough but not too much. Always remind me that words are very powerful and I must be careful with what comes out of my mouth. Today I ask for Your help in controlling my words. Cause my communication to be pleasing to You and encouraging to others. Amen."

Don't use foul or abusive language. Let everything you say be good and helpful, so that your words will be an encouragement to those who hear them.
Ephesians 4:29 NLT

DAY 44
Community

"*Lord*, help me to surround myself with a loving community of people. Help me to understand that life was not meant to be lived alone but alongside others. Cause me to be willing to sacrifice whatever is necessary in order to stay active in a community of other believers. Amen."

And let us consider how we may spur one another on toward love and good deeds, not giving up meeting together, as some are in the habit of doing, but encouraging one another – and all the more as you see the day approaching.
Hebrews 10:24-25 NIV

DAY 45
Comparing

"*Lord*, help me to never give into the temptation of comparing myself to others. Cause me to strive to be the best me that I can be. Help me to understand that You have called everyone with a different calling. Amen."

Each one should test their own actions. Then they can take pride in themselves alone, without comparing themselves to someone else.
Galatians 6:4 NIV

DAY 46
Compassion

"*Lord*, give me a compassionate heart today for others who may not be as fortunate as I am. Help me to understand that we are all called to help others through tough times. Today give me enough of whatever I need to share with others. Amen."

*Bear one another's burdens,
and so fulfill the law of Christ.
Galatians 6:2 ESV*

DAY 47
Competence

"*Lord*, I know that You will never call me to do anything that You will not give me the competence to do. As I read Your Word today, cause me to see that if I have the will to obey Your Word, You will give me the power and ability to do it. Amen."

So that the servant of God may be thoroughly equipped for every good work.
2 Timothy 3:17 NIV

DAY 48
Compensation

"*Lord*, help me to understand how much You want to bless Your kids. The Bible teaches that in eternity we will be compensated for our works done on this earth. It also teaches us in the sow and reap law that we reap some consequences now in this life. Help me to recognize Your involvement in many of the blessings in my life today and give You thanks. Amen."

Remember that the Lord will reward each one of us for the good we do, whether we are slaves or free.
Ephesians 6:8 NLT

DAY 49
Competition

"*Lord*, help me to understand that sometimes I have to compete with other people in life for things, whether it be in my career, recreational sports, or business. But always remind me that good character is more important than winning. Deliver me today from a spirit of competition. Amen."

Do nothing from selfish ambition or conceit, but in humility count others more significant than yourselves.
Philippians 2:3 ESV

DAY 50
Complaining

"*Lord*, forgive me for ever complaining. Help me to understand that You are always working in my life to bring good even out of bad things. Give me the strength to show the world how much I trust in You by never complaining. Amen."

Do all things without grumbling or disputing.
Philippians 2:14 ESV

DAY 51
Compromise

"*Lord*, give me the courage to never compromise my godly values. Let me always hold true to my strong convictions in life no matter what the circumstances may be. Today help me not to compromise. Amen."

If you love Me, you will keep My commandments.
John 14:15 NASB

DAY 52
Condemnation

"*Lord*, thank You for the promise that I will never face condemnation for my sins. Every sin I have ever committed You have fully forgiven. Give me a spirit of praise and appreciation that Jesus paid the ultimate price for all my sins. Cause me to express that appreciation every day of my life. Amen."

There is therefore now no condemnation for those who are in Christ Jesus.
Romans 8:1 ESV

DAY 53
Confession

"*Lord,* help me to daily confess my sins to You in prayer. I need to be constantly reminded of where I need to change my behavior. Cause me to always be cognizant of my daily behavior so that my life might be more pleasing to You. Amen."

If we confess our sins, He is faithful and righteous to forgive us our sins and to cleanse us from all unrighteousness.
1 John 1:9 NASB

DAY 54
Confidence

"Lord, give me confidence today to believe that You are with me at all times. You will guide and lead me in this life, and then take me home to be with You when my life on this earth is over. Help me to radiate that confidence at all times. Amen."

Do not fear, for I am with you; do not anxiously look about you, for I am your God. I will strengthen you, surely I will help you, surely I will uphold you with My righteous right hand.
Isaiah 41:10 NASB

DAY 55
Confidentiality

"*Lord*, cause people to feel safe with me, and help me to never talk about things that others may share with me. Help me to live in such a way that people will be comfortable sharing their problems with me. Amen."

Whoever goes about slandering reveals secrets,
but he who is trustworthy in spirit keeps a thing covered.
Proverbs 11:13 ESV

DAY 56
Conflict

"Lord, cause me to never avoid conflict just because it might make me feel uncomfortable. Cause me to see that sometimes conflict is inevitable in life. Very often it provides me with opportunities to show Your love and power to others. Today help me to glorify You in my conflict. Amen."

So then we pursue the things which make for peace and the building up of one another.
Romans 14:19 NASB

DAY 57
Confusion

"*Lord*, cause me not to give up when I am confused. Just because I don't know the answer today to my dilemma doesn't mean that there isn't an answer. Cause me to trust You even when things are dark. Amen."

We are afflicted in every way, but not crushed; perplexed, but not driven to despair.
2 Corinthians 4:8 ESV

DAY 58
Conscience

"*Lord*, help me to understand that my conscience is connected to Your Holy Spirit who lives in me. Cause me to stay sensitive to what my conscience is trying to show me and to never allow it to become hardened. Today help me to live according to my conscience. Amen."

Whether you turn to the right or to the left, your ears will hear a voice behind you, saying, "This is the way; walk in it."
Isaiah 30:21 NIV

DAY 59
Consequences

"*Lord*, help me to see that with every action comes consequences. Godly behavior brings good consequences and ungodly behavior brings with it bad consequences. Cause me to always keep in mind that I must live with the consequences of my actions. Today teach me to seek You for wisdom in every decision I make. Amen."

Do not be deceived: God is not mocked, for whatever one sows, that will he also reap.
Galatians 6:7 ESV

DAY 60
Consistency

"*Lord*, help me today to know the things You have called me to do and give me the resolve to stay committed. Sometimes it is hard to be consistent in my devotion to You. Today I need Your divine power so that through consistency I might glorify You in these things. Amen."

Therefore, my beloved brothers, be steadfast, immovable, always abounding in the work of the Lord, knowing that in the Lord your labor is not in vain.
1 Corinthians 15:58 ESV

DAY 61
Contentment

"Lord, forgive me for complaining and always wanting more. Forgive me for not being more thankful for all the good things You have blessed me with. Today I need Your power to be content. Amen."

Not that I am speaking of being in need, for I have learned in whatever situation I am to be content.
Philippians 4:11 ESV

DAY 62
Control

"*Lord*, cause me to live in such a way that I don't always feel the need to be in control. Today give me the strength to cast my cares on You because I know You care for me, and to rest in the fact that You are ultimately in control of my life. Amen."

***Casting all your anxiety on Him,
because He cares for you.
1 Peter 5:7 NASB***

DAY 63
Convenience

"Lord, help me to not make convenience the top priority in my life. Give me the courage to give myself to the things You instruct me to do whether they are convenient or not. Help me to be willing to be inconvenienced for You. Amen."

Then Jesus said to His disciples, "If anyone wishes to come after Me, he must deny himself, and take up his cross and follow Me. For whoever wishes to save his life will lose it; but whoever loses his life for My sake will find it."
Matthew 16:24-25 NASB

DAY 64
Conversation

"*Lord*, cause my conversations to always be edifying to You and others. Help me to have the discipline to refrain from words that tear others down and discourage listeners in any way. Let all my conversations be filled with mercy and grace so that they might leave others encouraged and filled with faith. Amen."

Let no unwholesome word proceed from your mouth, but only such a word as is good for edification according to the need of the moment, so that it will give grace to those who hear.
Ephesians 4:29 NASB

DAY 65
Conviction

"Lord, cause me to understand that one of the many ways You talk to Your children is through the convictions of the heart. Today give me the strength and the courage to live by the convictions that You have placed within my heart. Amen."

*So I strive always to keep my
conscience clear before God and man.
Acts 24:16 NIV*

DAY 66
Correction

"*Lord*, today help me not to be too proud to receive constructive criticism in my life. Keep before me the fact that You saved me in order to change me, and I usually will not change unless I am made to feel uncomfortable about something in my life. Give me the grace today to embrace correction with a good attitude. Amen."

Whoever loves discipline loves knowledge, but he who hates reproof is stupid.
Proverbs 12:1 ESV

DAY 67
Culture

"*Lord*, open my eyes to see that our culture is not God-driven. Their ideas and philosophies are governed by ideologies that have not come from You. Give me the strength today to stand up for You and Your Word, and to not be afraid of being counter-cultural. Amen."

Do not be conformed to this world, but be transformed by the renewal of your mind, that by testing you may discern what is the will of God, what is good and acceptable and perfect.
Romans 12:2 ESV

DAY 68
Death

"*Lord*, remind me today that for Your children, death is not the end but the beginning. You promised us over and over again the gift of eternal life. Even if we die, we will live. Please remind me to rejoice in that truth today. Amen."

And everyone who lives and believes in Me will never die. Do you believe this?
John 11:26 NASB

DAY 69
Debt

"Lord, please give me the wisdom and the discipline to spend my money wisely. Let me know that getting into debt is a trick of the enemy to eventually wear me down and discourage me. Remind me that owning more and better things will not bring me happiness. Cause me to spend my money wisely. Amen."

Do not be one who shakes hands in pledge or puts up security for debts; if you lack the means to pay, your very bed will be snatched from under you.
Proverbs 22:26-27 NIV

DAY 70
Decisions

"*Lord*, help me to see that the way my life is turning out today is largely a result of the many decisions I have made over the years. Cause me to stop and pause today, and pray over the decisions I have to make, knowing that my future depends on it. Amen."

If any of you lacks wisdom, let him ask God, who gives generously to all without reproach, and it will be given him.
James 1:5 ESV

DAY 71
Dedication

"*Lord*, cause me to be dedicated to the things in life that are important. Help me to be willing to give some things up in order to be dedicated to the most important things. Cause me to see today that dedication to important things will demand that I say no to less important things. Amen."

Whatever you do, work heartily, as for the Lord and not for men.
Colossians 3:23 ESV

DAY 72

Deeds

"*Lord*, I know that someday I will be rewarded for my deeds on earth. Help my day to be full of good deeds. Cause me to see that most good deeds are made up of very small things. Help me to be an encourager, comforter, and giver to all those I meet today. Amen."

And let us not grow weary of doing good, for in due season we will reap, if we do not give up.
Galatians 6:9 ESV

DAY 73
Defeat

"Lord, today help me to redefine defeat in my life. If something happens in my life and causes me to be a far better person because of it, it may not be a totally bad thing. Cause me to be dedicated to squeezing a blessing out of every problem that comes my way. Nothing can completely defeat me unless I allow it. Amen."

And we know that God causes all things to work together for good to those who love God, to those who are called according to His purpose.
Romans 8:28 NASB

Fire Starters

DAY 74
Denial

"Lord, don't let me ever be ashamed of the fact that I belong to You. Don't let me ever deny You in any of my actions or words. Cause me to be very proud of the fact that I am a child of God, and You are my Heavenly Father. Amen."

***Like a muddied spring or a polluted fountain is a righteous man who gives way before the wicked.
Proverbs 25:26 ESV***

DAY 75
Depression

"*Lord*, cause me to understand that nothing can ever come into my life that You can't give me the strength to endure. Forgive me for always looking to other sources of healing before I look to You. Depression is not stronger than You, and if I seek You, You will show me a way through the dark valleys. Amen."

The righteous cry, and the LORD hears and delivers them out of all their troubles. The LORD is near to the brokenhearted and saves those who are crushed in spirit.
Psalm 34:17-18 NASB

DAY 76
Design

"*Lord*, I pray today that You will show me the reason I was put on this earth. You designed me for a special purpose. Please help me to understand that You designed me while I was in my mother's womb to do something special upon this earth. Amen."

For You formed my inward parts; You wove me in my mother's womb. I will give thanks to You, for I am fearfully and wonderfully made; wonderful are Your works, and my soul knows it very well.
Psalm 139:13-14 NASB

DAY 77
Desire

"*Lord*, You work in my life by planting desires in my heart. Give me a spirit of discernment to know the desires that have come from You and the ones that don't come from You. Amen."

For it is God who is at work in you, both to will and to work for His good pleasure.
Philippians 2:13 NASB

DAY 78
Despair

"*Lord*, help me to never give into despair. Cause me to realize that because You are my Heavenly Father I am never without hope. Help me to keep in mind that You are an all-powerful God, and that Your love for me is beyond my capability to comprehend. Today cause me to know that You are with me, and Your eyes are always on me. Amen."

We are hard pressed on every side, but not crushed; perplexed, but not in despair; persecuted, but not abandoned; struck down, but not destroyed.
2 Corinthians 4:8-9 NIV

DAY 79
Destiny

"*Lord*, help me to realize that You have promised heaven for all those who love You when they die. Cause that to always be my backdrop for every trial that comes my way. This earth is not my final resting place. The biggest part of my life is still ahead of me. Amen."

For here we have no lasting city, but we seek the city that is to come.
Hebrews 13:14 ESV

DAY 80
Determination

"*Lord*, cause me to be determined to never settle for less than what You have for me. Don't let me settle for whatever seems easy, but give me faith to hold on until You provide for me the better way. I need a fresh dose of determination. Amen."

For I know the thoughts that I think toward you, says the LORD, thoughts of peace and not of evil, to give you a future and a hope.
Jeremiah 29:11 NKJV

DAY 81
Devil

"*Lord*, remind me today that there is a real devil who is dedicated to my demise. Help me to not fall victim to his strategies to destroy me and everything precious in my life. Give me the power to defeat him today. Amen."

Be sober-minded; be watchful. Your adversary the devil prowls around like a roaring lion, seeking someone to devour.
1 Peter 5:8 ESV

DAY 82
Difference

"*Lord*, give me the opportunity today to make a difference in someone's life. Even if it's just an encouraging word or a short prayer with someone, let me be determined to be a difference maker today. Give me the opportunity to make a positive difference and bring value to those around me. Amen."

Therefore, as we have opportunity, let us do good to all people, especially to those who belong to the family of believers.
Galatians 6:10 NIV

DAY 83
Disagreement

"*Lord*, I know I will never agree with everyone on every subject, but cause me to have a great spirit regardless. Starting today teach me to agree to disagree with a fantastic attitude. Amen."

As for the one who is weak in faith, welcome him, but not to quarrel over opinions.
Romans 14:1 ESV

DAY 84
Disbelief

"*Lord*, don't let me ever be discouraged enough to stop believing. Constantly show me how to replenish my faith. Doubting is not a sin, but don't ever let my doubts turn into disbelief. Help me today to believe Your Word over and above what I feel and think. Amen."

Immediately the father of the child cried out and said, "I believe; help my unbelief!"
Mark 9:24 ESV

DAY 85
Discernment

"*Lord*, one of the fantastic gifts You have given me is the gift of discernment. It's the ability to know when something isn't right. With this gift I can avoid a lot of heartache that people with wrong motives can bring into my life. Today teach me to work on using this gift more. Amen."

Dear friends, do not believe everyone who claims to speak by the Spirit. You must test them to see if the spirit they have comes from God. For there are many false prophets in the world.
1 John 4:1 NLT

DAY 86
Discipline

"*Lord*, help me to keep in mind that most good things in life do not come to people who are not disciplined. It takes discipline and consistency to have a healthy body, good career, or good relationships. Today give me the courage to do what it takes to start disciplining myself in these areas so that I can obtain the reward. Amen."

Love not sleep, lest you come to poverty; open your eyes, and you will have plenty of bread.
Proverbs 20:13 ESV

DAY 87
Discrimination

"*Lord*, help me to never discriminate between people because they are different from me. Cause me to see everyone as being worthy of respect and honor. Today give me opportunities to show respect to every person I meet, and to not focus on our differences but on the fact that we are all Your creation. Amen."

For the whole law is fulfilled in one word: "You shall love your neighbor as yourself."
Galatians 5:14 ESV

DAY 88
Dishonesty

"Lord, I am very often surrounded by situations where I am tempted to be dishonest. I am tempted to cheat on my taxes, tell little white lies, and sugarcoat things in order to make my life easier. Today please help me to be honest, with a spirit of love and understanding. Amen."

But speaking the truth in love, we are to grow up in all aspects into Him who is the head, even Christ.
Ephesians 4:15 NASB

DAY 89
Disobedience

"*Lord*, I believe in Your holy Word. Cause me to understand that obedience to it will bring me success. Today help me to see the areas where I am being disobedient, and give me the power to change. Amen."

So whoever knows the right thing to do and fails to do it, for him it is sin.
James 4:17 ESV

DAY 90
Disrespect

"*Lord*, disrespect has become a pretty common trait in our culture. Today cause me to see the need for a respectful attitude. Cause me to see a lot of little ways with which I can show respect to others. Amen."

Honor everyone. Love the brotherhood. Fear God. Honor the emperor.
1 Peter 2:17 ESV

DAY 91
Distraction

"*Lord*, this world is designed to distract us. Social media, television, music, and recreation can all serve as distractors in our lives. They can keep us from really important things like hearing Your voice, spending time with family and friends, and serving You. Help me identify the things in my life that have come to distract me. Amen."

Let your eyes look straight ahead; fix your gaze directly before you. Give careful thought to the paths for your feet and be steadfast in all your ways.
Proverbs 4:25-26 NIV

DAY 92

Doors

"*Lord*, cause me to always be aware of all the open doors that come my way. Help me to identify them and to take advantage of them when they come. Amen."

For a wide door for effective work has opened to me, and there are many adversaries.
1 Corinthians 16:9 ESV

DAY 93

Dreams

"*Lord*, make me a dreamer. Plant dreams in my heart and mind. Cause me to see that You have called me to accomplish great things in life. Your calling is bigger than the small world I have created for myself. Today make me a dreamer that I might accomplish Your will for my life. Amen."

And God spoke to Israel in visions of the night and said, "Jacob, Jacob." And he said, "Here I am."
Genesis 46:2 ESV

DAY 94
Easter

"*Lord*, Easter brought with it the best news that man has ever received. There is no more power in death for those who belong to You. I want to thank You today, more than just once a year, for giving us the message of Easter that we have victory over death. Amen."

He is not here, for He has risen, just as He said. Come, see the place where He was lying.
Matthew 28:6 NASB

DAY 95
Elderly

"*Lord*, the elderly are very often a forgotten group of people. Today show me ways to honor the elderly, and to make sure they know that they are important and not forgotten. Amen."

*Gray hair is a crown of glory;
it is gained in a righteous life.
Proverbs 16:31 ESV*

DAY 96
Embarrassment

"*Lord*, cause me to know that embarrassing situations are inevitable in life. Help me to never feel that any one situation defines my life. Help me to learn to laugh at myself and realize that not everyone gets it right all the time. Amen."

Judge not, that you be not judged.
Matthew 7:1 ESV

DAY 97

Embracing

"*Lord*, cause me to see that I need to embrace the things in my life that happen to help me grow. No matter how uncomfortable they are, if they have the potential of making me more like Jesus, then help me to embrace them and look for the blessing. Amen."

Consider it all joy, my brethren, when you encounter various trials, knowing that the testing of your faith produces endurance. And let endurance have its perfect result, so that you may be perfect and complete, lacking in nothing.
James 1:2-4 NASB

DAY 98
Emotion

"*Lord*, help me to understand that You created us with emotions. Emotions are good for many reasons, but they need to be controlled. Today give me the strength to use my emotions for good and to not let them control me. Amen."

A fool gives full vent to his spirit, but a wise man quietly holds it back.
Proverbs 29:11 ESV

DAY 99
Empathy

"*Lord*, help me try to imagine what I would feel if I was living in another person's shoes. Then help me to do something to lessen their pain and hurt. Let me work on this until it becomes a habit. Amen."

Rejoice with those who rejoice, weep with those who weep.
Romans 12:15 ESV

DAY 100
Empty

"*Lord*, help me to empty myself so I might be filled. Help me not to be afraid of giving out what I have in service to You, knowing that You will give back. Like a sponge that can't receive more water until it empties itself of the water it is carrying, help me to understand that You have created me to give so that I might receive. Amen."

Whoever has a bountiful eye will be blessed, for he shares his bread with the poor.
Proverbs 22:9 ESV

DAY 101
Encouragement

"Lord, help me to encourage everyone I meet today, knowing that what I give out to others comes back to me. Cause me to look for a silver lining in every trial that comes my way. Help me to believe that You cause all things to work together for good when we love You and are called according to Your purpose. Amen."

And we know that God causes all things to work together for good to those who love God, to those who are called according to His purpose.
Romans 8:28 NASB

DAY 102
Endurance

"*Lord*, the Bible tells me that faith needs to be combined with endurance in order to receive promises from You. Please help me to be patient while I wait for You to answer my prayers. Amen."

For you have need of endurance, so that when you have done the will of God you may receive what is promised.
Hebrews 10:36 ESV

DAY 103
Enemies

"*Lord*, help me to realize that I have both spiritual and physical enemies in the world who want to bring me down and discourage me. Today cause me to know that You are my source of victory and my defender. Amen."

Be strong and courageous. Do not fear or be in dread of them, for it is the Lord your God who goes with you. He will not leave you or forsake you.
Deuteronomy 31:6 ESV

DAY 104
Energy

"*Lord*, today I need You to supply me with the energy I need to accomplish Your will for my life. Cause me to pray for energy, eat right for energy, and sleep well so that I can do my best in serving You. Amen."

Strengthened with all might, according to His glorious power, for all patience and longsuffering with joy.
Colossians 1:11 NKJV

DAY 105
Enjoyment

"*Lord*, help me enjoy the many blessings that You have given me today. Cause me to not take any of them for granted. Let my day be filled with the joy that You provide. Amen."

There is nothing better for a person than that he should eat and drink and find enjoyment in his toil. This also, I saw, is from the hand of God.
Ecclesiastes 2:24 ESV

DAY 106
Enthusiasm

"*Lord*, help me to understand that without a spirit of enthusiasm my life will never be as productive as I want it to be. Today renew my enthusiasm for all the things that You have called me to do. Amen."

Whatever you do, do your work heartily, as for the Lord rather than for men.
Colossians 3:23 NASB

DAY 107
Eternity

"*Lord*, cause me to understand that You never planned for this earth to be my forever home. Let me see everything in my life through the lens of eternity. My real life will only begin once I leave this earth. Amen."

For God so loved the world, that He gave His only begotten Son, that whoever believes in Him shall not perish, but have eternal life.
John 3:16 NASB

DAY 108

Ethics

"*Lord*, give me the wisdom to base all my ethics on Your holy Word. You are our creator. You made us, and You fully understand the kind of life we should live in order to have abundant life. Today cause me to trust You with the outcome of an ethical life. Amen."

All Scripture is breathed out by God and profitable for teaching, for reproof, for correction, and for training in righteousness, that the man of God may be complete, equipped for every good work.
2 Timothy 3:16-17 ESV

DAY 109
Evangelizing

"*Lord*, help me see the need to tell everyone about Your goodness and grace. Cause the actions of my life to speak louder than my words. Today help me spread the good news about You and Your kingdom. Amen."

And He said to them, "Go into all the world and preach the gospel to every creature."
Mark 16:15 NKJV

DAY 110
Exaggeration

"*Lord*, cause me to understand that constant exaggeration can cause me to lose my integrity with others. Today help me not to see a need to exaggerate in my conversations. Amen."

*Deliver me, O Lord, from lying lips,
from a deceitful tongue.
Psalm 120:2 ESV*

DAY 111
Example

"*Lord*, today give me the power to be an example of what a Christian should be in everything I do and say. Cause me to always be asking myself, 'What would Jesus do in this situation? How would He respond if He were here?' Help me to model the life of Christ today. Amen."

Dear brothers and sisters, pattern your lives after mine, and learn from those who follow our example.
Philippians 3:17 NLT

DAY 112
Exercise

"*Lord*, help me to take good care of the body You have given me. Always remind me that in order for me to please You on this earth and carry out Your will for my life, I must have a healthy body. Today give me the discipline to exercise and eat a healthy diet. Amen."

Therefore I urge you, brethren, by the mercies of God, to present your bodies a living and holy sacrifice, acceptable to God, which is your spiritual service of worship.
Romans 12:1 NASB

DAY 113

Excess

"Lord, today show me any areas of my life where I am out of balance. Am I being excessive in any area beyond reason? Help me today to not be excessive in my appetite, speech, spending, or hobbies. Help me to be pleasing to You in all of these areas. Amen."

Everyone who competes in the games exercises self-control in all things. They then do it to receive a perishable wreath, but we an imperishable.
1 Corinthians 9:25 NASB

DAY 114
Excuses

"*Lord*, free me from having to use excuses all the time instead of being able to speak the truth in love. Help me to have the courage to live according to my conscience. Cause me to see that the constant use of excuses can become a form of dishonesty and can become habit-forming. Today give me the strength to be honest in my replies to others. Amen."

But they all alike began to make excuses. The first said to him, "I have bought a field, and I must go out and see it. Please have me excused." And another said, "I have bought five yoke of oxen, and I go to examine them. Please have me excused." And another said, "I have married a wife, and therefore I cannot come."
Luke 14:18-20 ESV

DAY 115

Failure

"*Lord*, give me the strength to handle failure in a godly way. Everyone fails in many ways. Failure cannot defeat me if I learn from it and grow in the area I failed in. Help me today not to be a slave to my failures. Amen."

And He has said to me, "My grace is sufficient for you, for power is perfected in weakness." Most gladly, therefore, I will rather boast about my weaknesses, so that the power of Christ may dwell in me. Therefore I am well content with weaknesses, with insults, with distresses, with persecutions, with difficulties, for Christ's sake; for when I am weak, then I am strong.
2 Corinthians 12:9-10 NASB

DAY 116

Faith

"*Lord*, help me to become a person of faith. Today cause me to see beyond my circumstances and to focus on You, knowing that You are bigger and more powerful than any situation that may come my way. Cause me today to find a promise in Your Word and to stand on it. Amen."

Now faith is the assurance of things hoped for, the conviction of things not seen.
Hebrews 11:1 ESV

DAY 117

Family

"*Lord*, today I thank You for my family. Give me the opportunity before the day is over to reach out to them and tell them how much they mean to me, and how thankful I am that God gave them to me. Cause me to never take my family for granted. Amen."

Your wife will be like a fruitful vine within your house; your children will be like olive shoots around your table.
Psalm 128:3 ESV

Listen to your father who gave you life, and do not despise your mother when she is old.
Proverbs 23:22 ESV

DAY 118

Fear

"*Lord*, help me today with all of my fears. Reassure me that no matter what I may go through, You will go through it with me. Give me promises from Your Word to hold onto, and cause my mind to dwell on these promises more than the things I fear. Amen."

Fear not, for I am with you; be not dismayed, for I am your God. I will strengthen you, yes, I will help you, I will uphold you with My righteous right hand.
Isaiah 41:10 NKJV

DAY 119
Feelings

"Lord, give me the strength I need to keep my feelings in check. Cause me to understand that feelings can work for me or against me. Help me to understand that my feelings are to be under my control and not to be controlling me. Amen."

We destroy arguments and every lofty opinion raised against the knowledge of God, and take every thought captive to obey Christ.
2 Corinthians 10:5 ESV

DAY 120
Fellowship

"*Lord*, today help me to see that there are a lot of fellows in the same ship with me. Cause me to stay in contact with my fellow brothers and sisters in Christ. Help me to see that they all have a role to play in my life, and they are holy conduits through which the Spirit of Christ flows. Amen."

So encourage each other and build each other up, just as you are already doing.
1 Thessalonians 5:11 NLT

DAY 121
Fidelity

"*Lord*, today help me to keep my mind pure and cause me to carefully guard everything that I allow to come into my life. Give me the discernment to know what music, media, and habits I should entertain, and which ones I need to exclude from my life in order to be pure. Amen."

Flee from sexual immorality. Every other sin a person commits is outside the body, but the sexually immoral person sins against his own body.
1 Corinthians 6:18 ESV

DAY 122
Finances

"*Lord*, cause me today to be wise with my finances. Help me see that it is a trick of our spiritual enemy to get us into financial debt. He will tempt us to spend money unwisely. Don't let us ever become the victim of financial debt, but give us the wisdom we need to invest wisely. Amen."

The rich rules over the poor, and the borrower is the slave of the lender.
Proverbs 22:7 ESV

DAY 123
First Love

"*Lord*, today help me to remember what it was like when I first discovered You. Bring me back to that place of excitement and simplicity that I first experienced in my earlier years. Help me to do what I did then in order to recapture that first love that I once had. Amen."

But I have this against you, that you have abandoned the love you had at first. Remember therefore from where you have fallen; repent, and do the works you did at first.
Revelation 2:4-5 ESV

DAY 124

Fitness

"*Lord*, today cause me to see physical exercise in the light of spiritual duty. Give me the discipline I need to keep the earth suit You have given me in good shape. Amen."

Don't you realize that your body is the temple of the Holy Spirit, who lives in you and was given to you by God? You do not belong to yourself.
1 Corinthians 6:19 NLT

DAY 125

Flesh

"*Lord*, help me today to see that I am engaged in a war between my body with its fleshly desires, and my spirit who is connected to You. They both struggle to control my life. Give me the power today to feed the spirit more than I feed my flesh. Amen."

The mind governed by the flesh is death, but the mind governed by the Spirit is life and peace.
Romans 8:6 NIV

DAY 126

Food

"*Lord*, cause me to understand that as Your vessel, I have a responsibility to eat healthy foods. Today give me the wisdom and the desire to replace the unhealthy foods in my home with healthy substitutes. Cause me to see the role that eating healthy plays in my life. Amen."

And God said, "Behold I have given you every plant yielding seed that is on the face of all the earth, and every tree with seed in its fruit. You shall have them for food."
Genesis 1:29 ESV

DAY 127
Forgetting

"Lord, help me to understand that there are many things in life that I need to forget. Many of my past failures, sins committed against me, and bad things that have happened to me are just a few things that I need to let go of. Today give me the gift of forgetting in reference to these areas. Amen."

Jesus replied, "No one who puts a hand to the plow and looks back is fit for service in the kingdom of God."
Luke 9:62 NIV

DAY 128

Forgiveness

"*Lord*, if I want to be forgiven, I need to forgive. Help me to be a person who forgives others. Cause me to see that the pain others have caused me may never go away, but I have the power to set them free from what they have done to me. Never let me forget the many times I have hurt others in my life, and show me the need to do for others what I would like done for myself. Today remind me of anyone I have not forgiven. Amen."

Be kind to one another, tender-hearted, forgiving each other, just as God in Christ also has forgiven you.
Ephesians 4:32 NASB

DAY 129
Forsaken

"*Lord*, I thank You because of the promise in Your Word that says I will never be forsaken. No matter what dark valley I go through, I know You will go through it with me. Today cause me not to be afraid of anything that might come in the future. Amen."

Even though I walk through the valley of the shadow of death, I fear no evil, for You are with me; Your rod and Your staff, they comfort me.
Psalm 23:4 NASB

DAY 130
Freedom

"Lord, I know that there is great freedom in my walk with You. Please help me to never take advantage of my freedom in Christ, but cause me to always be willing to give up my rights for the sake of others. Today show me the places and times when I need to give up my rights so that others may be blessed. Amen."

For you were called to freedom, brothers. Only do not use your freedom as an opportunity for the flesh, but through love serve one another.
Galatians 5:13 ESV

DAY 131
Friends

"*Lord*, please help me to choose my friends wisely. Cause me to understand the importance of having the right friends. The wrong friends can bring me down and cause me to walk in a wrong direction, and the right friends will help me to succeed in life. Today show me the friendships I need to nourish and the ones I need to let go. Amen."

Do not be deceived: "Bad company ruins good morals."
1 Corinthians 15:33 ESV

DAY 132
Fruitfulness

"*Lord*, today help me to bear spiritual fruit. Always remind me that the spiritual fruit I produce today can become a blessing to myself and others in the future. The people I lead to the Lord and the ministries I become a part of have the potential to be a huge blessing later on in life. Today cause me to sow seeds with a view of the future. Amen."

That person is like a tree planted by streams of water, which yields its fruit in season and whose leaf does not wither – whatever they do prospers.
Psalm 1:3 NIV

DAY 133
Funerals

"*Lord*, cause me to understand that we all must die someday. Today help me to start living in such a way that people will have a lot of good things to say at my funeral. Amen."

It is better to go to the house of mourning than to go to the house of feasting, for this is the end of all mankind, and the living will lay it to heart.
Ecclesiastes 7:2 ESV

DAY 134

Future

"*Lord*, what I do today has a lot to do with how my future turns out. Cause every decision I make today to be made with the future in mind. Free me from the temptation to cast the future aside and only live for the pleasure of today. Today is the first day of the rest of my life. Help me to live it wisely. Amen."

The plans of the diligent lead surely to abundance, but everyone who is hasty comes only to poverty.
Proverbs 21:5 ESV

DAY 135

Giving

"Lord, help me to never be so careful with my money that I become a stingy person who only uses my money for myself. Help me understand that everything I have belongs to You, because I belong to You. Thank You for letting me use a lot of it to supply my own needs and desires, but don't let me ever forget those who are less fortunate. Amen."

In everything I showed you that by working hard in this manner you must help the weak and remember the words of the Lord Jesus, that He Himself said, "It is more blessed to give than to receive."
Acts 20:35 NASB

DAY 136
Gloating

"*Lord*, I need Your help to stay humble at all times. Help me to see that everything I have and everything I am is a product of Your grace. Keep gloating far from me, and convict me every time that I begin to think too highly of myself. Amen."

Let another praise you, and not your own mouth; a stranger, and not your own lips.
Proverbs 27:2 ESV

DAY 137
Goals

"Lord, give me the wisdom to be able to understand why You put me on this earth. Cause me to set some goals that will help me to achieve Your will for my life. Let me see that setting goals is an important part of being successful in life. Help me to write out some short-term and long-term goals today. Amen."

So teach us to number our days that we may get a heart of wisdom.
Psalm 90:12 ESV

DAY 138
Gossip

"*Lord*, today give me the power over the sin of gossip. Cause me to always ask myself why people need to know what I am tempted to tell them. Also help me not to listen to gossip. Constantly remind me that I am to treat others as I would want to be treated, and I would not want to be the victim of malicious gossip. Today help me to be sensitive to what comes out of my mouth and what I listen to. Amen."

A gossip goes around telling secrets, but those who are trustworthy can keep a confidence.
Proverbs 11:13 NLT

DAY 139
Government

"*Lord*, help me to pray for all the leaders who serve in our government. Show me that I am to pray for them more than I criticize them. Help me to be an example to others of how we should have a respect for the position these men and women hold. Amen."

Everyone must submit to governing authorities. For all authority comes from God, and those in positions of authority have been placed there by God.
Romans 13:1 NLT

DAY 140

Grace

"*Lord*, I thank You for Your grace. It is the undeserved favor that comes from You. There is no way that I can live a perfect life. I will always disappoint You and myself in many ways. Cause me to see that Your grace will always cover all of my shortcomings. Today help me not to focus on my mistakes as much as Your awesome grace, and remind me to never forget that it is by the gift of grace that I stand righteous in Your sight. Amen."

For by grace you have been saved through faith. And this is not your own doing; it is the gift of God, not a result of works, so that no one may boast.
Ephesians 2:8-9 ESV

DAY 141
Gratification

"*Lord*, You have made all the good things in life to enjoy. Today help me to gratify myself with those good things that You have given me and find my happiness in them. Cause me not to chase after the things of the world in order to find gratification. What You have already given me is enough. Amen."

As for the rich in this present age, charge them not to be haughty, nor to set their hopes on the uncertainty of riches, but on God, who richly provides us with everything to enjoy.
1 Timothy 6:17 ESV

DAY 142

Greatness

"Lord, help me to redefine what greatness is. The Bible teaches us that greatness is found in becoming a servant to others. When I help others achieve their spiritual goals in life, I please You. Help me today not to strive to be great in the world's eyes but to be great in Your eyes. Show me how to serve today. Amen."

It shall not be so among you. But whoever would be great among you must be your servant.
Matthew 20:26 ESV

DAY 143
Greed

"Lord, free me from the spirit of greed. Cause me to see that earthly possessions can never satisfy, but only when I am pleasing to You will I find satisfaction in everything I already have. Don't let me confuse greed with ambition. Today show me anything in my life that I feel I cannot live without, and cause me to give that to You. Please refocus my desires. Amen."

And He said to them, "Take heed and beware of covetousness, for one's life does not consist in the abundance of the things he possesses."
Luke 12:15 NKJV

DAY 144
Grief

"*Lord*, I trust You to help me when I am grieving over the loss of someone precious in my life. My hope is in the overwhelming power of Your Spirit. Let me know that You will never fail me in my moments of grief, but You will draw near to me as I call upon Your mighty name. Nothing is ever lost when it is in Your hands. Please cause me to focus beyond this world today. Amen."

But we do not want you to be uninformed, brethren, about those who are asleep, so that you will not grieve as do the rest who have no hope. For if we believe that Jesus died and rose again, even so God will bring with Him those who have fallen asleep in Jesus.
1 Thessalonians 4:13-14 NASB

DAY 145
Growth

"*Lord*, it is my natural tendency to stop growing. In order to grow I know I must continue in the things that promote spiritual growth like prayer, studying the Word, and having fellowship with other believers. Today show me where I need to rededicate myself in order to continue to grow spiritually. Amen."

But grow in the grace and knowledge of our Lord and Savior Jesus Christ. To Him be the glory, both now and to the day of eternity.
2 Peter 3:18 NASB

DAY 146

Grudges

"*Lord*, help me to never hold grudges against anyone who has done anything to me. If You have forgiven me for all the dumb things I have done against You, then the least I can do is forgive others for the dumb things they have done that have hurt me. Please show me anyone today that I may be holding a grudge against, and give me the power to forgive. Amen."

Let all bitterness and wrath and anger and clamor and slander be put away from you, along with all malice. Be kind to one another, tenderhearted, forgiving one another, as God in Christ forgave you.
Ephesians 4:31-32 ESV

DAY 147
Grumbling

"*Lord*, I know that it is not pleasing to You when I grumble and complain about things. When I grumble and complain, I am making a statement to the world about Your love and goodness directed towards me. Today please help me catch myself when I am tempted to grumble or complain, and turn that issue into a prayer instead. Amen."

Do all things without grumbling or disputing, that you may be blameless and innocent, children of God without blemish in the midst of a crooked and twisted generation, among whom you shine as lights in the world.
Philippians 2:14-15 ESV

DAY 148

Guidance

"*Lord*, I need the guidance of Your Holy Spirit each and every day. Today cause me to be familiar with Your voice, Your Word, and Your ways so that I might not be led astray. You would have never told me that You would guide me if it wasn't within my power to follow. Today help me to order my life after the convictions of Your Spirit and Your Word. Amen."

Trust in the LORD with all your heart and do not lean on your own understanding. In all your ways acknowledge Him, and He will make your paths straight.
Proverbs 3:5-6 NASB

DAY 149
Guilt

"Lord, give me discernment to distinguish between conviction and guilt. Help me to understand that conviction goes away once I confess my sins to You and try to make restitution, whereas guilt lingers. When I confess my sins, You are faithful to forgive me. Cause me today to refuse to let guilt weigh me down. Amen."

Therefore, there is now no condemnation for those who are in Christ Jesus.
Romans 8:1 NIV

DAY 150

Habits

"*Lord*, don't let bad habits ruin my life. Cause me to see that You have given me the strength to overcome bad habits and replace them with good habits. Today help me to identify the things in my life that need to change, and show me good things I can put in their place. Amen."

"All things are lawful for me," but not all things are helpful. "All things are lawful for me," but I will not be dominated by anything.
1 Corinthians 6:12 ESV

DAY 151

Happiness

"Lord, help me to see that happiness comes and goes, but the joy of the Lord remains. Happiness rises and falls with circumstances, but the joy of the Lord comes from the indwelling of the Holy Spirit. Help me today to pursue joy over happiness. Amen."

You will make known to me the path of life; in Your presence is fullness of joy; in Your right hand there are pleasures forever.
Psalm 16:11 NASB

DAY 152
Hard Work

"*Lord*, help me not to be lazy. Cause me to see that good things come to those who are not afraid to put some effort into their labors. Today show me areas of my life that I need to work harder at, and give me the strength to be diligent and consistent in those areas, keeping my eyes on the reward. Amen."

The soul of the sluggard craves and gets nothing, while the soul of the diligent is richly supplied.
Proverbs 13:4 ESV

DAY 153
Hatred

"*Lord*, help me today to make a decision not to hate anyone. Make me aware of the fact that people are going to treat me badly all throughout life, and although I can't keep that from happening, I can control the way I react to it. Please show me how to forgive those who have hurt me, and help me move on. Amen."

Whoever says he is in the light and hates his brother is still in darkness.
1 John 2:9 ESV

DAY 154
Healing

"Lord, cause me to see that You are my healer. Remind me to bring every physical, spiritual, and emotional need to You in prayer, that I might receive wisdom, guidance, and healing in my time of need. Amen."

The LORD nurses them when they are sick and restores them to health.
Psalm 41:3 NLT

DAY 155
Hearing God

"*Lord*, cause me to understand that there are many ways I can hear Your voice. You are speaking when I am convicted about things, You are speaking to me every time I hear an anointed sermon, You are speaking to me every time I read Your Word, and You are speaking to me when I listen to worship music. Today please help me to hear what You are saying to me. Amen."

And your ears shall hear a word behind you, saying, "This is the way, walk in it," when you turn to the right or when you turn to the left.
Isaiah 30:21 ESV

DAY 156

Heaven

"*Lord*, I thank You for the awesome gift of eternal life that awaits me in heaven. Help me today to see heaven as the backdrop for every problem I go through. Cause me to never lose heart, knowing that this earth is not my final destination. Amen."

In My Father's house are many mansions; if it were not so, I would have told you. I go to prepare a place for you.
John 14:2 NKJV

DAY 157

Heresy

"*Lord*, help me to avoid far extremes and heresies. Cause me to recognize the teachings and philosophies that are not biblically-based. Help me to stay true to the sure foundation of Your Word. Amen."

Beloved, do not believe every spirit, but test the spirits to see whether they are from God, for many false prophets have gone out into the world.
1 John 4:1 ESV

DAY 158
Hoarding

"*Lord*, cause me to be a giver and not a hoarder. Let me always remember that I have been blessed in order to be a blessing. Today show me what I have that I am not using that can be a blessing to others. Amen."

For where your treasure is, there your heart will be also.
Luke 12:34 NIV

DAY 159
Hobbies

"*Lord*, help me to create some hobbies in my life so that I might have a more healthy, stress-free lifestyle. Cause me to see that having healthy hobbies is a part of Your plan for my life. Amen."

A person can do nothing better than to eat and drink and find satisfaction in their own toil. This too, I see, is from the hand of God.
Ecclesiastes 2:24 NIV

DAY 160

Holiness

"*Lord*, remind me that holiness just means that I am to be separated from the things in the world that keep me from doing Your will. Today show me anything in my life that is interfering with me doing Your will. Amen."

And you shall be holy to Me, for I the LORD am holy, and have separated you from the peoples, that you should be Mine.
Leviticus 20:26 NKJV

DAY 161
Honesty

"*Lord*, help me today to keep honesty as a top virtue in my life. Cause me to be aware of any little habits of dishonesty that have crept into my life unnoticed. Amen."

For we aim at what is honorable not only in the Lord's sight but also in the sight of man.
2 Corinthians 8:21 ESV

DAY 162
Honor

"*Lord*, cause me to always give honor to those who honor is due. Cause me to honor all those in authority, the elderly, and those who are placed in a position over me. Today let me be an example to others by honoring those who deserve honor. Amen."

Likewise, you who are younger, be subject to the elders. Clothe yourselves, all of you, with humility toward one another, for "God opposes the proud but gives grace to the humble."
1 Peter 5:5 ESV

DAY 163
Honoring God

"*Lord*, today I want to recognize Your power over all things. We live in a society that has no respect for Your name. You are our creator, sustainer, and our provider. Let me never forget to honor You in everything I do and say. Show me any areas of my life where I am not living in a reverent way or acknowledging Your lordship. Amen."

Whether, then, you eat or drink or whatever you do, do all to the glory of God.
1 Corinthians 10:31 NASB

DAY 164

Hope

"*Lord*, let me know that I never need to lose hope as long as I have You in my life. Just because I can't see You moving in my life does not mean that You aren't. Today help me to remember that You are bigger than any problem I may be facing. Let me put my trust in Your great love and concern for me, so that others may see my confidence and be drawn to You. Amen."

Now may the God of hope fill you with all joy and peace in believing, so that you will abound in hope by the power of the Holy Spirit.
Romans 15:13 NASB

DAY 165
Hospitality

"*Lord*, help me today to rediscover the power of hospitality. Remind me how important it is to show people Your love in a relaxed, tranquil environment. Today let me discover new ways to use my home as a tool to touch people with Your love. Amen."

Show hospitality to one another without grumbling.
1 Peter 4:9 ESV

DAY 166

Houses

"*Lord*, show me how to make my house into a home. Cause my house to become a sanctuary for my family from the stresses of the world and its daily pressures. Today show me anything I need to change in order to make my house a more stress-free and loving environment. Amen."

By wisdom a house is built,
and by understanding it is established.
Proverbs 24:3 ESV

DAY 167
Humanity

"*Lord*, help me to never expect more out of myself than I was made to give. Remove from me the pressure to always be right and to never fail. Cause me to see my humanity, and to understand that I have never been called to perfection. The most godly women and men down through the ages of time have made many mistakes and failed in many ways. No human being was ever perfect. Today help me to accept myself along with all of my quirks and insufficiencies. Amen."

Blessed are the poor in spirit,
for theirs is the kingdom of heaven.
Matthew 5:3 ESV

DAY 168
Humility

"*Lord*, help me to constantly see myself as You see me. Cause me to see others as more important than myself. Help me to see that everything I have and everything I have become is because of Your grace and great love extended towards me. I am nothing without You. Please keep me humble. Amen."

True humility and fear of the LORD lead to riches, honor, and long life.
Proverbs 22:4 NLT

DAY 169
Humor

"*Lord*, constantly remind me to not take life so seriously all the time. Give me the grace to see life through a humorous lens. Give me the power to be able to laugh at myself. Today free me from the bondage of always having to have a sober and contrite spirit. Laughter is good for the soul. Supply me with a lot of opportunities today to laugh. Amen."

A joyful heart is good medicine, but a crushed spirit dries up the bones.
Proverbs 17:22 ESV

DAY 170
Hunger

"*Lord*, keep my soul hungry for You and Your Word. Put a strong desire in my heart for godliness. Today stir up within me a desire to do the things necessary to keep growing and changing. Amen."

Blessed are those who hunger and thirst for righteousness, for they shall be satisfied.
Matthew 5:6 ESV

DAY 171
Hypocrisy

"Lord, show me any areas in my life where I live in hypocrisy. Let me not be afraid of living in a transparent way before my loved ones and peers. Cause me to see that I never need to be afraid of being me, and I never have to wear a mask for anyone. Help me to be comfortable in my skin today. Amen."

Beware of practicing your righteousness before other people in order to be seen by them, for then you will have no reward from your Father who is in heaven.
Matthew 6:1 ESV

DAY 172

Identity

"*Lord*, help me to find my identity in You. It is a huge thing to be called a child of God. Let me always remind myself that I belong to You and will someday live forever in Your kingdom. Amen."

But as many as received Him, to them He gave the right to become children of God, even to those who believe in His name.
John 1:12 NASB

DAY 173
Idleness

"Lord, I need to always understand that idleness can become an enemy of my soul. I need to take regular time-outs in order to revitalize my soul and my body, but I must beware lest I let them turn into seasons of idleness. As long as I am on this earth, there will be a lot of kingdom work for me to do. Today show me the things You have called me to do on this earth in my short years that I am here, and cause me to never become the victim of idleness. Amen."

For we hear that some among you walk in idleness, not busy at work, but busybodies.
2 Thessalonians 3:11 ESV

DAY 174

Idolatry

"*Lord*, show me anything in my life that may get in the way of loving You. Don't let me put anything in front of my dedication to doing Your will on this earth. Keep me from every form of idolatry. Amen."

Therefore, my beloved, flee from idolatry.
1 Corinthians 10:14 ESV

DAY 175
Ignorance

"*Lord*, help me to be a continual learner of Your Word and Your ways. Let me have no excuse for spiritual ignorance as long as I have a Bible to learn from. Today cause me to set aside a time and a place to study Your Word. Amen."

For, being ignorant of the righteousness of God, and seeking to establish their own, they did not submit to God's righteousness.
Romans 10:3 ESV

DAY 176
Illness

"*Lord*, comfort me in my time of illness, and cause me to be there for others during their times of illness. Help me today to reach out to those who are sick, to pray for them, and help them in any way I can to get them through this time of trial in their life. Cause me not to be too busy to lend a helping hand. Amen."

I was naked and you clothed Me; I was sick and you visited Me; I was in prison and you came to Me.
Matthew 25:36 NKJV

DAY 177
Immorality

"*Lord*, we live in a very immoral culture and environment in our world today. Please help me to keep all of my thoughts and ways pure in Your sight. Help me to have strong values in my life in regards to social media and entertainment. Cause me to model a life of purity and to never be ashamed of my counter-cultural values. Cause me to be aware of any areas today where I may be failing in my endeavors and pursuit of morality. Amen."

But sexual immorality and all impurity
or covetousness must not even be named among you,
as is proper among saints.
Ephesians 5:3 ESV

DAY 178
Immortality

"*Lord*, I cannot fathom the idea of immortality. The fact that I am going to live forever and ever in Your kingdom totally blows my mind. Daily when life gets tough I need to remind myself of that. Thank You so much for giving me the gift of immortality. Amen."

For the wages of sin is death, but the free gift of God is eternal life in Christ Jesus our Lord.
Romans 6:23 ESV

DAY 179
Impatience

"*Lord*, help me with my impatient attitude. Cause me to call upon Your Holy Spirit to help me in times of impatience. Help me to understand the Spirit's role in supplying me with the strength I need to be patient. Patience is not something that I am naturally inclined towards. Today when I am tempted to lose my patience, remind me to call upon Your Spirit to give me the supernatural ability to be able to be the person You want me to be. Amen."

Whoever is patient has great understanding, but one who is quick-tempered displays folly.
Proverbs 14:29 NIV

DAY 180

Imperfection

"Lord, help me not to be ashamed of my physical imperfections. You created me exactly as I am. There is only one of me on this earth. Please help me to never compare myself to others, but to accept myself the way I am. Amen."

But the LORD said to Samuel, "Do not look on his appearance or on the height of his stature, because I have rejected him. For the LORD sees not as man sees: man looks on the outward appearance, but the LORD looks on the heart."
1 Samuel 16:7 ESV

DAY 181
Impossibility

"*Lord*, nothing is impossible for You! Help me to never view any problem outside of Your ability to solve it. You created the world with a spoken word. Cause me to remove the word 'impossibility' from my vocabulary today. Amen."

Jesus looked at them and said, "With man this is impossible, but with God all things are possible."
Matthew 19:26 NIV

DAY 182

Increase

"*Lord*, in the Bible I am told that my job is to plant seeds in life, and it is up to You to cause the increase. No matter whether I plant financial seeds, seeds of kindness, or seeds of the gospel, if I plant them in Your name, You will cause there to be an increase in whatever I plant. Thank You for that promise today. Amen."

Now he who supplies seed to the sower and bread for food will also supply and increase your store of seed and will enlarge the harvest of your righteousness.
2 Corinthians 9:10 NIV

DAY 183
Independence

"*Lord*, help me to see my dependence upon others in the body of Christ. I was never made to go through life alone, but life was made from the very beginning to be lived alongside others. Help me to never be ashamed to reach out to others for help in time of need. Amen."

The eye cannot say to the hand, "I don't need you!" And the head cannot say to the feet, "I don't need you!"
1 Corinthians 12:21 NIV

DAY 184
Inheritance

"*Lord*, help me to keep my eyes on the inheritance that is laid up for me in heaven. Cause me not to envy people who are rich in this world, but to realize that my inheritance still awaits me after I die. Because of what awaits me in heaven, I don't need to build my kingdom here on this earth. Help me to think on these things today. Amen."

Whatever you do, work heartily, as for the Lord and not for men, knowing that from the Lord you will receive the inheritance as your reward.
You are serving the Lord Christ.
Colossians 3:23-24 ESV

DAY 185
Insecurity

"*Lord*, I praise You that I never have to be insecure when I have You in my life. You have promised to make ALL things work together for good for those who love You and are called according to Your purpose. You have also promised to be with me and never leave me. When I am tempted with feelings of insecurity, please give me a promise of Your Word to hold on to. Amen."

For I know the plans I have for you, declares the Lord, plans for welfare and not for evil, to give you a future and a hope.
Jeremiah 29:11 ESV

DAY 186
Inspiration

"*Lord*, today remind me that to be inspired by You, I need to stay close to You. You are the giver of inspiration. Many great things have been accomplished in this world through inspired ideas that came from You. Cause me to be inspired by You as I spend quiet time in Your Word and prayer. Birth ideas and thoughts in my mind that were not there before! Amen."

But it is the spirit in man, the breath of the Almighty, that makes him understand.
Job 32:8 ESV

DAY 187
Instruction

"*Lord*, help me to understand that You have left us with instructions in Your Word about how to have a prosperous walk with You. You have left instructions that deal with marriage, money, raising children, health, and many more things. When I follow those instructions, I have success, and when I don't, I often fail. Please teach me the value of not only reading the Word and studying it but also obeying it. Today let me not be too busy to read the instructions. Amen."

I will instruct you and teach you in the way which you should go; I will counsel you with My eye upon you.
Psalm 32:8 NASB

DAY 188
Integrity

"*Lord*, teach me to be a person who is the same both in the light and in the darkness. Show me any inconsistencies in who people think I am and who I really am. Cause me to live according to my inner convictions and according to my conscience at all times. Today give me opportunities to practice living in integrity. Amen."

Better is a poor man who walks in his integrity than a rich man who is crooked in his ways.
Proverbs 28:6 ESV

DAY 189
Intimidation

"*Lord*, help me to never be intimidated by the enemy. I must make up my mind to never shrink back in fear when You have called me to do something. The devil will try to intimidate me by putting doubts and fearful thoughts in my mind in order to keep me from doing what You have instructed me to do. Give me the power to never fear the outcome of obeying You. Amen."

For God gave us a spirit not of fear but of power and love and self-control.
2 Timothy 1:7 ESV

DAY 190

Intoxication

"*Lord*, give me the strength to avoid intoxication, knowing that Your Word speaks strongly against it. Cause me to always keep in mind all the lives that have been destroyed by the misuse of alcohol, and cause me to be an example of righteousness in this area. Show me today how I can stay free from becoming a victim of intoxication. Amen."

Wine produces mockers; alcohol leads to brawls. Those led astray by drink cannot be wise.
Proverbs 20:1 NLT

DAY 191
Investing

"*Lord*, teach me how to be a wise investor while I am on this earth. Let me know that every day I am given opportunities to invest in heavenly rewards. Every kind deed I do, every encouraging word I give, every person I lift up in prayer, every one of these actions will someday be rewarded in heaven. Today make me a wise investor. Amen."

But lay up for yourselves treasures in heaven, where neither moth nor rust destroys and where thieves do not break in and steal.
Matthew 6:20 ESV

DAY 192
Irresponsibility

"*Lord*, there are many things You have entrusted into my care. Cause me to be responsible with caring for my family by spending time with them. Cause me to be responsible with my finances and spend my money wisely. Cause me to be responsible with caring for the needs of the church that You have made me a part of. Today show me any areas in my life where I might be irresponsible. Amen."

Therefore, to one who knows the right thing to do and does not do it, to him it is sin.
James 4:17 NASB

DAY 193
Irritable

"*Lord*, every day I experience things that irritate me. Life very rarely will go my way. Help me today to find a way to not let unpleasant things get the best of me. Give me the power to respond instead of reacting. Cause me to smile more and to keep my critical opinions to myself, lest I slowly become an irritable person that no one wants to be around. Amen."

*A fool always loses his temper,
but a wise man holds it back.
Proverbs 29:11 NASB*

DAY 194
Jealousy

"*Lord*, help me to never be jealous of others. Cause me not to compare what I have with what others have. Cause me to be content with what You have given me and not always be wanting more. Let me understand that everyone is traveling down a different road and will be given different things for reasons we will never understand. Today help me to be happy for others instead of being jealous. Amen."

A peaceful heart leads to a healthy body; jealousy is like cancer in the bones.
Proverbs 14:30 NLT

DAY 195
Journey

"*Lord*, we are all on a journey in this world that is leading to our spiritual destination. Help us today not to be ashamed to ask for wisdom and counsel from people who have been on this journey longer than us, knowing that their advice can save us a lot of heartache. Cause us today to take advantage of the wise people You have put in our lives. Amen."

The way of a fool is right in his own eyes, but a wise man listens to advice.
Proverbs 12:15 ESV

DAY 196
Judgmentalism

"*Lord*, cause me today to not judge people who are different than me. Save me from always having to feel like everyone must do things my way or else they are wrong. Set me free from trying to be You in other people's lives. Help me to not always have to have an opinion on everything. Amen."

A fool takes no pleasure in understanding, but only in expressing his opinion.
Proverbs 18:2 ESV

DAY 197
Justification

"Lord, cause me to always take responsibility for my actions and to not fall into the habit of justification. Help me to see any areas of my life that I may be justifying today. Cause me to replace justification with confession and repentance. Let me have a glimpse of how powerful the gift of transparency can be. Amen."

The man replied, "It was the woman you gave me who gave me the fruit, and I ate it."
Genesis 3:12 NLT

DAY 198

Kids

"*Lord*, help me to see kids as you see them.
You see our children as little future disciples given into
our care to be trained and then sent out into the world.
Help me today to see clearly what I may need to change
in order to help my kids grow into the people
You want them to be. Amen."

*Behold, children are a heritage from the LORD, the fruit
of the womb a reward. Like arrows in the hand of a
warrior are the children of one's youth. Blessed is the man
who fills his quiver with them! He shall not be put to
shame when he speaks with his enemies in the gate.
Psalm 127:3-5 ESV*

DAY 199
Kindness

"*Lord*, cause me to realize that Scripture says that Your kindness leads people to repentance. Repentance is a change of heart or opinion. Today give me the wisdom and the opportunities to show people Your kindness through a word, a gesture, or a small gift. Cause me to do it in Your name so I can show others Your kindness, and hopefully they will have a change of opinion about You. Amen."

Or do you think lightly of the riches of His kindness and tolerance and patience, not knowing that the kindness of God leads you to repentance?
Romans 2:4 NASB

DAY 200

Laziness

"*Lord*, help me to never give in to a spirit of laziness. Cause me to see that there is no excuse for being lazy. Help me to carry my share of the load in my home and at work, as well as in the church. Show me any areas where I need to do more. Amen."

Whatever you do, work at it with all your heart, as working for the Lord, not for human masters.
Colossians 3:23 NIV

DAY 201
Learning

"*Lord*, cause me to see that every day I should be desiring to learn new things. At the end of every day, I should reflect back on what I learned that day. Give me the desire to keep a journal and write down all the things that I am learning each and every day. Today cause me not to waste my time by allowing my mind to dwell on mundane, unimportant things. Help me to ask questions and be a learner, so when I am older I will be a person of wisdom. Amen."

Let the wise hear and increase in learning, and the one who understands obtain guidance.
Proverbs 1:5 ESV

DAY 202

Lessons

"Lord, help me to reframe how I see failure. If I learn a great lesson out of my failure and the result is that I become a better person because of it, then it wasn't totally a bad thing. Cause me today to understand that some lessons in life will only be learned through failure. Help me not to move on from the failure until I have learned a lesson from it. Amen."

But the Helper, the Holy Spirit, whom the Father will send in My name, He will teach you all things, and bring to your remembrance all that I said to you.
John 14:26 NASB

DAY 203
Listening

"*Lord*, help me to be a better listener. In a world where everyone is concerned more about what they have to say than what they are hearing others say, we need listeners. When we listen to other people, we cause them to feel loved and important. Today remind me to listen more than I talk. Amen."

Understand this, my dear brothers and sisters: You must all be quick to listen, slow to speak, and slow to get angry.
James 1:19 NLT

DAY 204
Loneliness

"*Lord*, there are a lot of lonely people on this earth. Help me to understand that not everyone has significant people in their lives who care about them. Help me to reach out to those people and be there for them, even if it's just a text or a short call to let them know that I care. Then teach me that this is the solution for my loneliness, for whatever I do for others will come back to me. Today make me aware of any lonely people in my life. Amen."

Turn to me and be gracious to me,
for I am lonely and afflicted.
Psalm 25:16 ESV

DAY 205
Longevity

"*Lord*, bless me with a long, fruitful life. Don't let me die until my work here on earth is done. Let me see that there are things I need to do in order to have longevity. Help me today to eat right, deal with the stress in my life, exercise, and to develop good sleep habits. Also cause me to find Your will for my life. All of these things will help me have a life of longevity. Help me today to see if I am lacking in any area. Amen."

Wisdom will multiply your days
and add years to your life.
Proverbs 9:11 NLT

DAY 206

Losing

"*Lord*, help me learn how to be a good loser. Life is not about winning all the time. Oftentimes we can influence people for God more by being a great loser than a winner. Cause me to see that when I lose, my attitude in life says more about me than receiving the accolades of being a winner. Anyone can win and have a great attitude, but true character is on display when we lose. Help me to be a great loser today. Amen."

We are careful to be honorable before the Lord, but we also want everyone else to see that we are honorable.
2 Corinthians 8:21 NLT

DAY 207

Love

"*Lord*, cause me to understand that there is nothing greater in this world than my love for You and my love for others. Cause me to see that the primary way I show my love to You is by loving Your people. You taught us in Your Word that what we do for others we do for You. Today give me opportunities to feed You, to encourage You, to pray for You, and to help You, always keeping in mind that whatever I do for others I do for You. Help me to show my love for You today. Amen."

And above all these put on love, which binds everything together in perfect harmony.
Colossians 3:14 ESV

DAY 208
Lowly

"*Lord*, don't ever let me begin to think that I am better than others and become exclusive about who I hang out with. Cause me to see that those in the world that are more lowly in society are very loved by You. I can learn much from these people as well as others. Don't let me ever think I am too good to associate with the lowly. Amen."

Pride goes before destruction, and a haughty spirit before a fall. It is better to be of a lowly spirit with the poor than to divide the spoil with the proud.
Proverbs 16:18-19 ESV

DAY 209

Lukewarm

"*Lord*, show me how to stay passionate about my love for You and Your people. Don't let me become lukewarm in my dedication to You. Today give me the discipline to do the things necessary that will feed my soul and passion. Amen."

I know all the things you do, that you are neither hot nor cold. I wish that you were one or the other!
Revelation 3:15 NLT

DAY 210

Lust

"*Lord*, help me today to control my lusts of the flesh. Show me how to discipline my mind when I see it lusting after things I should not have. Unbridled lust, if not controlled, can lead to my downfall and defeat. Today show me when I begin to lust for wrong things. Give me the discipline to cast that thought aside immediately, acknowledging its ultimate power to destroy me and everything precious in my life. Amen."

For all that is in the world – the desires of the flesh and the desires of the eyes and pride of life – is not from the Father but is from the world.
1 John 2:16 ESV

DAY 211
Lying

"*Lord*, keep me from letting little innocent white lies creep into my life. Help me to be careful to always tell the truth. Today show me any areas of my life that I have let become undisciplined by condoning these little white lies. Help me to break those habits, and show me how to rechannel those lies with loving transparency. Amen."

Do not lie to one another, seeing that you have put off the old self with its practices and have put on the new self, which is being renewed in knowledge after the image of its creator.
Colossians 3:9-10 ESV

DAY 212

Manners

"*Lord*, help me to see that good manners will open doors for me to have influence in some people's lives that I may not have had otherwise. Teach me to always be polite to everyone I meet, because I never know the role they could play in my life later on. Good manners are a part of loving others. Cause me today to be cognizant of how I am coming off to other people. Amen."

Do to others as you would have them do to you.
Luke 6:31 NIV

DAY 213
Marriage

"Lord, cause me to see that my marriage reflects the relationship of Christ and the church. Today help me to understand that I am to make my spouse one of the most important people in my life. Cause me not to take them for granted. Remind me that they are a blessing from You, and that I made a vow when I married them to love them for better or worse. Cause me to fulfill that vow today, and show me ways to love my spouse more. Amen."

However, let each one of you love his wife as himself, and let the wife see that she respects her husband.
Ephesians 5:33 ESV

DAY 214
Materialism

"Lord, keep me from making things more important than people. Cause me to see that my life is not defined by how much I own, but by how much I love. Help me to never fall prey to sacrificing relationships for the pursuit of more money and things. Help me today to recognize any areas in my life where I might be becoming materialistic. Amen."

Then He said to them, "Beware, and be on your guard against every form of greed; for not even when one has an abundance does his life consist of his possessions."
Luke 12:15 NASB

DAY 215
Maturity

"*Lord*, help me to learn to grow up in all areas of my life. If there are any areas of my life where I am childish or immature, cause me to become aware of those areas so I can change. Cause me to see that maturity requires me to sometimes give up on having things my way so others can be blessed. Amen."

Brothers, do not be children in your thinking. Be infants in evil, but in your thinking be mature.
1 Corinthians 14:20 ESV

DAY 216
Mean People

"Lord, cause me to see that mean people are unhappy people. You have called me to love everyone and that includes mean people. Help me to understand that I have been given Your divine power to help me love the unlovable. If I don't show them love, who will? Today give me the courage to show mean people Your love. Amen."

For the anger of man does not achieve the righteousness of God.
James 1:20 NASB

DAY 217
Meditation

"Lord, You gave me the gift of meditation, so help me to take advantage of it. Help me to understand the power of spiritual revelation that comes when I meditate on Your Word. Today help me to take advantage of this great gift. Amen."

This book of the law shall not depart from your mouth, but you shall meditate on it day and night, so that you may be careful to do according to all that is written in it; for then you will make your way prosperous, and then you will have success.
Joshua 1:8 NASB

DAY 218

Meekness

"*Lord*, help me to always keep my emotions under control. Cause me to be in charge of my actions, my tongue, and my temper. Today help me to call upon Your Spirit to help me when I am tempted to lose control. Amen."

They must not slander anyone and must avoid quarreling. Instead, they should be gentle and show true humility to everyone.
Titus 3:2 NLT

DAY 219

Memories

"*Lord*, help me to be diligent to make a lot of memories with my friends, family, and loved ones. When I am gone from this earth, let the memories I made live on. Cause me to never stop living and making memories. Amen."

I thank my God every time I remember you.
Philippians 1:3 NIV

DAY 220

Miracles

"Lord, don't let me ever stop believing in miracles. Don't ever let me give up hope in any situation. The Bible teaches me that I have not because I ask not, so let me ask big when I have a need. I never know when I might receive a miracle. I will not receive a miracle if I don't believe they are possible. Help me to never stop believing. Amen."

He said to them, "Because of your little faith. For truly, I say to you, if you have faith like a grain of mustard seed, you will say to this mountain, 'Move from here to there,' and it will move, and nothing will be impossible for you."
Matthew 17:20 ESV

DAY 221
Missions

"Lord, we are all called to live a missional life no matter where we reside. While we do appreciate and support those who have given up a lot of modern conveniences to travel abroad, we must also not lose sight of the missional work all around us. There are foster kids who need homes, elderly people who have been forgotten, and hungry people in our communities. Show me today how to be a missionary in my own community. Amen."

And He said to them, "Go into all the world and preach the gospel to all creation."
Mark 16:15 NASB

DAY 222
Mistakes

"*Lord*, today help me to remember that because I am human I will make mistakes. My job is not to be perfect but to be righteous. A righteous person admits their mistakes and tries to do better next time. Today don't let me focus on my mistakes as much as I focus on what I do after I make the mistake. Help me to be humble today. Amen."

Indeed, we all make many mistakes.
James 3:2 NLT

DAY 223
Modesty

"*Lord*, help me today to leave my pride at home. Cause me to not be overly proud of the car I drive, the clothes I wear, or my title in life. Cause me not to put emphasis on outdoing the others around me. Give me a spirit of modesty. Amen."

So, whether you eat or drink, or whatever you do, do all to the glory of God.
1 Corinthians 10:31 ESV

DAY 224

Money

"*Lord*, give me enough money to be able to meet the basic needs of life and have some left over to give to charitable causes. Help me to focus on the things that money can't buy. Cause me to see that a walk in the park, playing with my child, making a meal with my family and laughing, or attending a church service, are things that cost nothing. These things are more important than anything that money can buy. Today supply me with enough money to meet my needs, but not so much that I would lose focus of the more important things in life. Amen."

No one can serve two masters, for either he will hate the one and love the other, or he will be devoted to the one and despise the other. You cannot serve God and money.
Matthew 6:24 ESV

DAY 225
Moral Absolutes

"Lord, help me to understand that You are God, and You have the right to establish moral absolutes for Your people. Cause me to study the Bible to see what those are and to be obedient to Your commands. Help me to keep in mind that the people who don't acknowledge You as God will not agree with the moral absolutes that I center my life around. Give me the strength today to stand boldly and unashamedly for my godly morals. Amen."

Woe to those who call evil good and good evil, who put darkness for light and light for darkness, who put bitter for sweet and sweet for bitter!
Isaiah 5:20 ESV

DAY 226
Morality

"*Lord*, cause me to understand the concept of morality. It is basically a system of determining right and wrong or good and bad behavior. Today help me to always be asking myself the question, 'What would Jesus do in this particular situation?' Cause me to have the heart of Christ as I go into the world today. Amen."

So whatever you wish that others would do to you, do also to them, for this is the Law and the Prophets.
Matthew 7:12 ESV

DAY 227

Mothers

"*Lord*, today cause us to take a moment to appreciate our mothers. Help us to not always have to wait for Mother's Day or a birthday to reach out and tell them how much we appreciate their place in our life. Some things are more meaningful when they are not expected. So today prompt me to send a text, write a letter, send a card, or even make a phone call to express my love for my mom. Amen."

Strength and dignity are her clothing, and she laughs at the time to come. She opens her mouth with wisdom, and the teaching of kindness is on her tongue. She looks well to the ways of her household and does not eat the bread of idleness. Her children rise up and call her blessed; her husband also, and he praises her: "Many women have done excellently, but you surpass them all."
Proverbs 31:25-29 ESV

DAY 228
Mourning

"*Lord*, help me to learn how to mourn. The Bible teaches us Christians that we should mourn, but not as those who have no hope. Our mourning as believers should somehow reflect the hope of Christ and His promises to us. Today help me to mourn with a purpose in mind. Cause me to know when my season of mourning should be over, and I should move on. Give me the grace to mourn as one who has hope for the future. Amen."

Blessed are those who mourn, for they shall be comforted.
Matthew 5:4 ESV

DAY 229
Mouth

"*Lord*, today I need Your help in controlling what comes out of my mouth. Don't let me not say enough, but also don't let me say too much. Help me to have the right words for each particular situation I come across today. Cause me to see that sometimes fewer words are better. Thoughtful, encouraging words with a smile can mean more than anyone could ever imagine. Help me to use my tongue wisely to build up and encourage everyone I see. Amen."

Set a guard over my mouth, Lord; keep watch over the door of my lips.
Psalm 141:3 NIV

DAY 230
Moving On

"*Lord*, help me to know when it's time to move on from certain situations in my life. Today show me the places in my life where I need to close an old chapter and start writing a new one. Give me the courage I need to say goodbye to this season and hello to another. Help me to refuse to stay in an unproductive rut. Amen."

Do not be overcome by evil, but overcome evil with good.
Romans 12:21 ESV

DAY 231
Music

"*Lord*, help me to understand how powerful music is, and help me to use it to my advantage. The Bible uses music, along with worship and praise, in many different instances and ways. We know that music has a strong influence on us and the spiritual realm. Today let me be very cognizant of the music that I entertain in my life. Amen."

He put a new song in my mouth, a song of praise to our God; many will see and fear and will trust in the Lord.
Psalm 40:3 NASB

DAY 232

Needs

"*Lord*, always remind me that You have promised in Your Word to supply all my needs. Don't let me confuse my needs with my desires. If You are not supplying what I see as a need, then let me understand that it might not be a need after all. Today show me what my needs really are. Amen."

Let them shout for joy and rejoice, who favor my vindication; and let them say continually, "The Lord be magnified, who delights in the prosperity of His servant."
Psalm 35:27 NASB

DAY 233
Neighbor

"Lord, reveal to me ways that I can show my neighbors the love of Christ. Cause me to never think that any act of kindness, as small as it may be, is too little for You to use. It may be a smile, a wave, an opportunity for a short prayer, or even lending someone a helping hand to move something from their car to the house. Help me today to be attentive to those opportunities, and to reach out and love my neighbors. Amen."

The second is this: "You shall love your neighbor as yourself." There is no other commandment greater than these.
Mark 12:31 ESV

DAY 234
Not Defeated

"*Lord*, help me to see defeat in the eyes of an eternal perspective. If I give something my best effort and it doesn't work out, that doesn't mean I experienced defeat. Quite possibly I grew some emotional, spiritual muscles in the situation that will serve me well in the future. Cause me to see defeat from Your perspective. Amen."

That the man of God may be complete, equipped for every good work.
2 Timothy 3:17 ESV

DAY 235
Obedience

"*Lord*, help me to realize that sometimes the destination of where You are leading me is not always clear. Teach me that simple obedience to what You have already told me to do is oftentimes the next step toward my destination. The Word of God is described as a lamp and not a spotlight. It often just shows me the next step. Today help me to obey what You are telling me to do and leave the rest to You. Amen."

If you are willing and obedient, you will eat the good things of the land.
Isaiah 1:19 NIV

DAY 236
Old Age

"Lord, cause me to honor the elderly realizing that someday I will be old. Help me to give them the respect they deserve and to always make myself aware of any needs they may have. Today cause me to take special notice of the elderly, and to express kindness to this often forgotten group of people. Amen."

You shall stand up before the gray head and honor the face of an old man, and you shall fear your God: I am the LORD.
Leviticus 19:32 ESV

DAY 237
Opinions

"*Lord*, help me to sometimes keep my opinions to myself. I don't need to always share what I feel to be true all the time. Today help me to be a sharer of the Word more than my opinions. Amen."

Now accept the one who is weak in faith, but not for the purpose of passing judgment on his opinions.
Romans 14:1 NASB

DAY 238
Optimism

"*Lord*, give me a positive attitude today. There is too much negativity in the world. Help me to look for something positive in every situation I encounter today. Amen."

Keep your heart with all vigilance, for from it flow the springs of life.
Proverbs 4:23 ESV

DAY 239
Organization

"*Lord*, help me to see the power of being organized. In the Bible, You had people get organized before You did the miracle of the fishes and loaves. Today cause me to see that I need to get all the clutter out of my life and become organized in my home and finances, so You can do more in my life. Amen."

Lazy people want much but get little, but those who work hard will prosper.
Proverbs 13:4 NLT

DAY 240
Our Past

"*Lord*, today cause me to realize that I can't change my past. It is what it is, but like the Apostle Paul said, I can choose to not let it impede my future. Every time my ugly past comes into my mind let me make a diligent commitment to refuse to dwell on it. There is nothing good that can come out of reliving the awful details of my past failures, so today I will refuse the devil's attempts to remind me of what lies behind me. Amen."

Therefore if anyone is in Christ, he is a new creature; the old things passed away; behold, new things have come.
2 Corinthians 5:17 NASB

DAY 241
Our Weakness

"*Lord*, I am so aware of the weaknesses in my life. I ask You to forgive me for not coming to You for help in these areas and trying to fight them on my own. Today cause me to see that the Holy Spirit is my helper, and He is there to help me when I call upon Him in times of need. Remind me to come to You for help so that I don't have to fight alone. Amen."

And He said to me, "My grace is sufficient for you, for My strength is made perfect in weakness." Therefore most gladly I will rather boast in my infirmities, that the power of Christ may rest upon me.
2 Corinthians 12:9 NKJV

DAY 242
Overcoming

"*Lord*, the Bible says that those who are overcomers are blessed. An overcomer is someone who firmly believes that with You on their side nothing can ultimately defeat them. They have made up their mind to still be smiling when the dust settles, with the firm assurance that in the end You will make everything right. Help me today to put my total trust in You and to believe that because I love You, You will make all things right in the end. Amen."

For everyone who has been born of God overcomes the world. And this is the victory that has overcome the world – our faith.
1 John 5:4 ESV

DAY 243

Pain

"*Lord*, help me to see that sometimes pain is my friend and not my enemy. If I never felt pain, I would often continue to do things that were harming me. Instead of taking all pain away from me, teach me what to do with it. Today show me how to turn my pain into gain. Amen."

Not only that, but we rejoice in our sufferings, knowing that suffering produces endurance, and endurance produces character, and character produces hope.
Romans 5:3-4 ESV

DAY 244

Parables

"*Lord*, the Bible uses a lot of parables. Parables were a very creative way to communicate in biblical days. They helped the listener better understand what was being said. Cause me today to see the power of using word pictures when I have very important things I need to communicate. Help me to be more effective and creative in my communication. Amen."

That it might be fulfilled which was spoken by the prophet, saying: "I will open My mouth in parables; I will utter things kept secret from the foundation of the world."
Matthew 13:35 NKJV

DAY 245

Parents

"*Lord*, today teach me what it is to be a great parent. Remind me that raising children is one of the most important things I will ever do. Every child starts out like a fresh lump of clay ready to be molded by the potter. Don't let me ever assume that I know everything about parenting. Today cause me to utilize all of the amazing resources that You have put around me to make me a better parent. Amen."

Train up a child in the way he should go; even when he is old he will not depart from it.
Proverbs 22:6 ESV

DAY 246
Parental Discipline

"Lord, don't let me be undisciplined in disciplining my children. Give me the wisdom I need to know how to discipline them wisely and with consistency. God, I confess that sometimes it is easier to ignore bad behavior than it is to take time out of my busy schedule to lovingly discipline my children. Today cause me to see that children don't grow up to be successful adults without proper discipline in their lives. Give me the strength to lovingly discipline my children. Amen."

Whoever spares the rod hates their children, but the one who loves their children is careful to discipline them.
Proverbs 13:24 NIV

DAY 247
Partiality

"Lord, help me to never show a spirit of partiality or to regard one person over another because of race, color, or social standing. Cause me to treat all people with dignity. Today cause me to be fully aware of any prejudices that might be in my life. Amen."

My brothers, show no partiality as you hold the faith in our Lord Jesus Christ, the Lord of glory.
James 2:1 ESV

DAY 248

Peace

"*Lord*, cause me to understand that when there is a lack of peace concerning any area of my life, I need to pray. Very often a lack of peace can be an indicator that I need to make some changes somewhere. Today cause me to be at peace with all areas of my life. Amen."

And let the peace of Christ rule in your hearts, to which indeed you were called in one body. And be thankful.
Colossians 3:15 ESV

DAY 249
People in Heaven

"*Lord*, remind me daily that heaven is a real place. Everything in our world is built of 3 basic building blocks: protons, electrons, and neutrons. You have many building blocks that go far beyond the physical realm, and heaven is a real place in one of these other domains. Keep reminding me that my loved ones who died in Christ are very much alive in heaven awaiting my arrival someday. Cause me to never lose sight of that awesome fact. Amen."

And He said to him, "Truly I say to you, today you shall be with Me in Paradise."
Luke 23:43 NASB

DAY 250

Perseverance

"Lord, let me see that as Christians we are called to persevere in times of trial. Cause me to understand that whereas endurance is to hold our ground, perseverance is to continue making forward progress in spite of our difficulty. Today give me the courage not to stop doing what You have called me to do regardless of the discomfort it may cause me. Amen."

Let us not lose heart in doing good, for in due time we will reap if we do not grow weary.
Galatians 6:9 NASB

DAY 251

Plans

"Lord, help me to always let my plans be secondary to Your plans. When I have to change my plans because of Your will for my life, cause me not to grumble. Today cause me to submit all my plans to You in prayer and trust Your will to be better than mine. Amen."

"For I know the plans I have for you," says the LORD. "They are plans for good and not for disaster, to give you a future and a hope."
Jeremiah 29:11 NLT

DAY 252
Pleasure

"*Lord*, help me to understand that living for You is one of the best ways to live a quality life on this earth. Our spiritual enemy will try to make us believe that we are giving up on all the pleasures in this life if we surrender our lives to doing God's will on earth. Help us to never believe that lie. While we are called to live a holy life and will be called to give up many pleasures of this world, living in Your presence and doing Your will on this earth is still the best life a person can live. Amen."

You will show me the path of life; in Your presence is fullness of joy; at Your right hand are pleasures forevermore.
Psalm 16:11 NKJV

DAY 253
Popularity

"*Lord*, help me to never make popularity more important than being holy. Help me to understand that there will be times when You will call me to make decisions that will not be popular with everyone. Cause me today to see character as being more important than popularity. Amen."

The fear of man lays a snare, but whoever trusts in the LORD is safe.
Proverbs 29:25 ESV

DAY 254
Potential

"*Lord*, help me to strive to reach my potential in life. Don't let me ever settle for a spirit of mediocrity. You created me with some awesome plans in mind. Help me to seek You in order to find out why You have me on this earth. Help me to reach my potential as a servant of Christ, as a parent, as a spouse, as a neighbor, and as a friend. Cause me to understand that in order to reach my potential, I will have to put out some effort. Show me today any areas in my life where I can do better. Amen."

Now to Him who is able to do far more abundantly beyond all that we ask or think, according to the power that works within us.
Ephesians 3:20 NASB

DAY 255
Poverty

"*Lord*, You have shown us that You have always had a heart for the poor. You have expressed Your love for them many times in the Bible. Today cause me to care about what You care about. Show me the legitimately poor people that I may come across, and help me to never have a closed heart to helping them in any way I can. Amen."

Open your mouth for the mute, for the rights of all who are destitute. Open your mouth, judge righteously, defend the rights of the poor and needy.
Proverbs 31:8-9 ESV

DAY 256
Power of Prayer

"*Lord*, cause me to always remember that the Bible says that the prayer of a righteous person accomplishes much. It doesn't promise me that it will change all of my circumstances. A mountain is moved by one rock at a time. Today help me to be consistent in my prayers knowing that I am gradually making progress each and every day that I pray. Amen."

Never stop praying.
1 Thessalonians 5:17 NLT

DAY 257
Power of Testimony

"*Lord*, let me never underestimate the power of my testimony. I was once blind, but now I see. Please cause me to see that we all have a testimony. We all had a different life before we decided to start following Christ. Cause me to use my story in order to help others. Amen."

And with great power the apostles were giving their testimony to the resurrection of the Lord Jesus, and great grace was upon them all.
Acts 4:33 ESV

DAY 258
Power of God

"*Lord*, Your power is made available to Your children on earth. We can tap into Your power through prayer, using our spiritual authority, and obeying Your Word. Lord, today cause me to become a student of Your power. Give me opportunities to use Your power in my life. Amen."

Jesus looked at them intently and said,
"Humanly speaking, it is impossible. But with God
everything is possible."
Matthew 19:26 NLT

DAY 259
Praying for Others

"Lord, help me to see my responsibility to pray for others knowing that prayer works. The Bible teaches that we have not because we ask not. When we are asked to pray for someone, help us to keep in mind that we might pray something that nobody else will pray. Today cause me to depend upon the Holy Spirit to know how to pray for others. Amen."

I urge you, first of all, to pray for all people. Ask God to help them; intercede on their behalf, and give thanks for them.
1 Timothy 2:1 NLT

DAY 260
Predestination

"Lord, the Bible teaches us that we are predestined to be conformed to the image of Jesus Christ. Today You will be working on changing me. Help me to always be asking myself the question: 'Does this situation have the potential to create in me any godly characteristics? Will it make me more humble, more relatable, or more sympathetic?' Help me to embrace the things that make me more like Christ. Amen."

For those whom He foreknew, He also predestined to become conformed to the image of His Son, so that He would be the firstborn among many brethren.
Romans 8:29 NASB

DAY 261
Prejudice

"Lord, sometimes when we think of being prejudice we just think of racial prejudices, but it is so much more than that. Today show me if I have a prejudice spirit related to racial, social, or even economic status. Show me any group of people that I hold in low esteem, and please start a healing process in that area. Help me to love everyone the same no matter how different they are than me. Show me that I don't have to like certain things about a person in order to love them. Amen."

There is neither Jew nor Greek, there is neither slave nor free, there is no male and female, for you are all one in Christ Jesus.
Galatians 3:28 ESV

DAY 262
Presence of God

"*Lord*, help me to live in Your presence. Today help me to be disciplined and to spend time in Your Word, prayer, and worship. It's only then that I will hear Your voice and feel Your presence. Amen."

You will make known to me the path of life; in Your presence is fullness of joy; in Your right hand there are pleasures forever.
Psalm 16:11 NASB

DAY 263
Priorities

"*Lord*, without a commitment to a set of priorities in my life, I will never become what You want me to be or have any real success in life. Today show me what is important in my life and what is not. Help me to dedicate myself to doing whatever is necessary to get the important things done. Give me the courage to say no to a lot of things that are not on my priority list, so that I might fulfill the things that are most important. Amen."

Put your outdoor work in order and get your fields ready; after that, build your house.
Proverbs 24:27 NIV

DAY 264
Protection

"Lord, let me look to You for protection for myself and my family. There are more things to be protected from than physical dangers. Protect us from the danger of backsliding, becoming proud, hanging around the wrong people, and even falling into the bondage of sin. Help me daily to look to You to be my protector. Amen."

But the Lord is faithful. He will establish you and guard you against the evil one.
2 Thessalonians 3:3 ESV

DAY 265
Provision

"*Lord*, You are my provider. Today give me everything I need to make it through this day. Help me to be able to distinguish between what I need and what I don't need. Give me the love I need to love everyone around me, the wisdom I need to make the right decisions, the power to not give in to sin, and enough grace to forgive those who sin against me. Amen."

And God is able to make all grace abound to you, so that having all sufficiency in all things at all times, you may abound in every good work.
2 Corinthians 9:8 ESV

DAY 266
Questions

"*Lord*, when I have questions that I don't have answers for, help me to trust in You. Cause me to know that as long as I am on this earth, I will have spiritual questions that I can't answer. Let me be okay with that. Help me today to realize that no one on this earth has answers to all of their questions. Just because I don't have an answer doesn't mean that there isn't an answer. Amen."

It is the glory of God to conceal a matter; to search out a matter is the glory of kings.
Proverbs 25:2 NIV

DAY 267

Quitting

"*Lord*, help me not to give up on things that I know I am suppose to be doing. Until You tell me to quit, I should never quit. It is okay to sometimes pause and take time to rest and refocus, but I must never quit until the job is done, or I am convinced that it is Your will to discontinue. Today infuse me with strength to continue. Amen."

Yet those who wait for the LORD will gain new strength; they will mount up with wings like eagles, they will run and not get tired, they will walk and not become weary.
Isaiah 40:31 NASB

DAY 268

Racism

"*Lord*, I pray today that You would keep me color blind. Help me to never see people according to their color or racial ethnicity. Cause me to see that everyone was born in Your image, and everyone should be treated the same. Amen."

Do not judge by appearances,
but judge with right judgment.
John 7:24 ESV

DAY 269
Raising Children

"Lord, cause me to understand that raising children is a lot of work if I do it right. Today help me to see any areas in my children's lives that are possibly being overlooked. Cause me to understand that I have been given the responsibility by You to raise them up to be productive adults in this world. I need Your strength to be willing to pay the price necessary to accomplish this job. Amen."

You shall teach them diligently to your children, and shall talk of them when you sit in your house, and when you walk by the way, and when you lie down, and when you rise.
Deuteronomy 6:7 ESV

DAY 270
Reading God's Word

"*Lord*, Your Word gives me wisdom for almost every challenge I face in life. Whether it's a financial need, marriage need, health issue, or a spiritual need, Your Word has something to say about it. Teach me to spend time in Your Word daily and to pray that You will give me understanding when I read. Today cause me to see the difference between reading and studying, and show me the tools I need to enhance my study time. Amen."

But He answered and said, "It is written, 'Man shall not live by bread alone, but by every word that proceeds from the mouth of God.'"
Matthew 4:4 NKJV

DAY 271
Real Love

"*Lord*, there are a lot of different kinds of love. There is a physical love, a love we have for our friends and relatives, and then there is Your kind of love. We call Your love agape love. It's the kind of love that is determined by our will and never expects anything in return. Today give me an opportunity to love people with Your kind of love. Help me to love the unlovable and those who have nothing to give back. Amen."

A new commandment I give to you, that you love one another: just as I have loved you, you also are to love one another.
John 13:34 ESV

DAY 272
Reap What You Sow

"*Lord*, let me decide what I need more of today, and then give me the opportunity to give some of that to others. Let me see the wisdom of living by the sow and reap law. Amen."

The point is this: whoever sows sparingly will also reap sparingly, whoever sows bountifully will also reap bountifully.
2 Corinthians 9:6 ESV

DAY 273

Reasons

"*Lord*, always cause me to see that I don't have to be given reasons for why I go through the things I go through. At those times when things don't make sense, cause me to trust that You are still in charge, and that You will see me through those times of trial. Help me to not have to have an answer before I start trusting You. Amen."

"For My thoughts are not your thoughts, nor are your ways My ways," declares the LORD. "For as the heavens are higher than the earth, so are My ways higher than your ways and My thoughts than your thoughts."
Isaiah 55:8-9 NASB

DAY 274
Reconciliation

"*Lord*, show me any relationships today that need mending in my life. As far as it depends on me, help me to live at peace with everyone. Give me the courage to be the initiator in any relationships that need to be healed. Amen."

Love prospers when a fault is forgiven, but dwelling on it separates close friends.
Proverbs 17:9 NLT

DAY 275
Recreation

"*Lord*, cause me to see that sometimes recreation can be Your will for my life. There will be times when I need to get away from everyday life in order to rest and refocus. Let me never feel guilty about taking time out to rest and have fun. Amen."

And He said to them, "Come aside by yourselves to a deserted place and rest a while." For there were many coming and going, and they did not even have time to eat.
Mark 6:31 NKJV

DAY 276
Reflection

"*Lord*, cause me to understand that as the moon reflects the sun, I am to reflect the image of Christ. After spending time with You, Moses was glowing from being in Your presence and wasn't aware of it. Today cause me to be filled with Your Spirit. Amen."

I have been crucified with Christ; and it is no longer I who live, but Christ lives in me; and the life which I now live in the flesh I live by faith in the Son of God, who loved me and gave Himself up for me.
Galatians 2:20 NASB

DAY 277
Regrets

"*Lord*, help me today to learn how to process and get closure on the things that have caused me regret in life. Let me understand that there is nothing I can do about those things now except extract a lesson from them and move on. Today help me make a decision to refuse to think about my regrets anymore. Amen."

Brothers, I do not consider that I have made it my own. But one thing I do: forgetting what lies behind and straining forward to what lies ahead, I press on toward the goal for the prize of the upward call of God in Christ Jesus.
Philippians 3:13-14 ESV

DAY 278
Regular Church Attendance

"*Lord*, help me to understand that church services are designed to keep me focused and spiritually strong. Help me to keep the practice of attending church a priority in life. Amen."

And they devoted themselves to the apostles' teaching and the fellowship, to the breaking of bread and the prayers.
Acts 2:42 ESV

DAY 279
Rejection

"*Lord*, no matter how hard I try, some people are going to reject me. Help me to expect this, knowing that my peace is always reflected by my expectations. Help me not to let it get me down. Amen."

If the world hates you, you know that it has hated Me before it hated you.
John 15:18 NASB

DAY 280
Rejoicing

"*Lord*, cause me to develop a habit of rejoicing. You have instructed me in Your Word to rejoice. It is simply an act of faith to express joy regardless of circumstances. Today help me to make a decision to express joy. Amen."

But be glad and rejoice forever in that which I create; for behold, I create Jerusalem to be a joy, and her people to be a gladness.
Isaiah 65:18 ESV

DAY 281
Relationships

"Lord, help me understand the power of relationships. Good relationships can enrich your life tremendously, and bad relationships can wreak havoc on your life. Today cause me to take inventory of the relationships I have in my life. Speak to me about the relationships that need to end and the ones that need to be nourished. Amen."

*A friend loves at all times,
and a brother is born for adversity.
Proverbs 17:17 ESV*

DAY 282
Relaxation

"Lord, cause me to learn how to occasionally turn off the stresses of the world and relax. There is healing and restoration in times of relaxation. This week help me to schedule a time to relax. Amen."

Be still, and know that I am God.
Psalm 46:10 ESV

DAY 283
Relevance

"Lord, show me how to stay relevant in our ever-changing society today. Staying relevant will help me to relate to people of all ages and promote Your kingdom. Staying relevant will require me to come to the understanding that even though Your Word never changes, the way society thinks and lives does change. Today give me the wisdom on how to be relevant and yet not compromise Your Word. Amen."

Let no one despise you for your youth, but set the believers an example in speech, in conduct, in love, in faith, in purity.
1 Timothy 4:12 ESV

DAY 284

Reliability

"Lord, I want You and others to be able to count on me as being a reliable person. I realize that in order to be reliable I need to keep my word. Starting today, help me to be careful with what I commit myself to, knowing that I have to keep those commitments in order to be reliable. Cause me to start working on being more reliable. Amen."

If you are faithful in little things, you will be faithful in large ones. But if you are dishonest in little things, you won't be honest with greater responsibilities.
Luke 16:10 NLT

DAY 285
Remembrance

"*Lord*, help me to use the gift of remembrance to my advantage. Starting today, help me to make sure that I am building a life of memories for those I love. Give me creative ideas of things I can do with my family and friends in order to build memories. Remind me to always take a lot of pictures so we can look back and remember. Today don't let me forget to remember. Amen."

The memory of the righteous is a blessing, but the name of the wicked will rot.
Proverbs 10:7 ESV

DAY 286
Renewing the Mind

"*Lord*, living in this world can clutter up my mind. Today cause me to be attentive to the wrong thoughts that I allow into my mind, and give me the power to not dwell on them. Renew my mind daily. Amen."

For those who live according to the flesh set their minds on the things of the flesh, but those who live according to the Spirit set their minds on the things of the Spirit. For to set the mind on the flesh is death, but to set the mind on the Spirit is life and peace.
Romans 8:5-6 ESV

DAY 287
Repentance

"Lord, give me the power and the will to turn away from everything in my life that I know isn't pleasing to You. I would probably stay stuck living in my sinful ways if it wasn't for the help of Your Holy Spirit. Today cause me to call upon Your Spirit to give me a heart of repentance. Amen."

From that time Jesus began to preach, saying, "Repent, for the kingdom of heaven is at hand."
Matthew 4:17 ESV

DAY 288
Reputation

"*Lord*, cause me to be less concerned about my reputation than I am about my character. My reputation has more to do with what people think about me and who they think I am, while my character is who I really am. Today help me not to come under bondage to my reputation, but cause me to be obedient to You regardless of what others may think. Amen."

Rather, he made himself nothing by taking the very nature of a servant, being made in human likeness.
Philippians 2:7 NIV

DAY 289
Resentment

"*Lord*, You are going to use others to occasionally correct me and chastise me. The Bible teaches that iron sharpens iron. Please help me not to resent those that You use in my life. Today show me anyone that I might feel resentful of so I can be healed. Amen."

See to it that no one comes short of the grace of God; that no root of bitterness springing up causes trouble, and by it many be defiled.
Hebrews 12:15 NASB

DAY 290
Resolving Conflict

"*Lord*, I need Your help in resolving conflict. I realize that the way I resolve conflict can either make me or break me. Teach me how to pray through every conflict I encounter and to control my emotions until things can be resolved. Help me not to be focused on who is right or wrong, but to keep as my goal a peaceful resolution. Amen."

*A soft answer turns away wrath,
but a harsh word stirs up anger.
Proverbs 15:1 ESV*

DAY 291
Restoring Friendships

"Lord, today remind me of any old friendships that may need to be renewed. Let me never forget that every quality relationship adds value to my life. Amen."

A man of many companions may come to ruin, but there is a friend who sticks closer than a brother.
Proverbs 18:24 ESV

DAY 292
Resurrection of Christ

"Lord, today I want to thank You for the awesome blessing that was brought about at the resurrection of Jesus Christ. Because of the resurrection, I have the blessed hope and confidence that I will never die. I also live with the awesome assurance that one day I will be reunited with all of my loved ones who have died in Christ. Thank You so much for this wonderful, blessed hope. Amen."

Blessed be the God and Father of our Lord Jesus Christ, who according to His great mercy has caused us to be born again to a living hope through the resurrection of Jesus Christ from the dead.
1 Peter 1:3 NASB

DAY 293
Revealing Secrets

"Lord, teach me how to keep a secret. To some degree, my integrity has a lot to do with my ability to keep a secret. For some people, their healing may depend upon them being able to reveal the ugly things that they have kept hidden in their hearts for years. These people need someone they can trust to listen to them and give them advice without the fear of someone gossiping about them. Help me to be a person that others can trust. Amen."

A gossip betrays a confidence, but a trustworthy person keeps a secret.
Proverbs 11:13 NIV

DAY 294

Revenge

"*Lord*, give me the wisdom to know how to respond when people do things to hurt me. Give me the courage and willpower to never take revenge into my own hands. Constantly remind me that You are always there to take up my cause and defend me. Help me today to trust in You. Amen."

Beloved, never avenge yourselves, but leave it to the wrath of God, for it is written, "Vengeance is mine, I will repay, says the Lord."
Romans 12:19 ESV

DAY 295

Reverence

"*Lord*, it seems like we are slowly losing our spirit of reverence on the earth for You and things that are holy. Cause me today to start modeling for others a spirit of reverence. Even if it's only taking off my hat when I pray or enter a holy place, kneeling at an appropriate time, or not walking down a church aisle when someone is praying, show me ways to become more reverent. Amen."

The fear of the Lord is the beginning of wisdom; all those who practice it have a good understanding. His praise endures forever.
Psalm 111:10 ESV

DAY 296
Rewards in Heaven

"*Lord*, You have told us in Your Word that we will be rewarded in heaven according to our works here on earth. Today help me to understand that life is a test in order to see what I will do with the talents and gifts You have given to me while I am on this earth. According to what I do with these talents, I will be rewarded in heaven. Today give me opportunities to use what little I have been given to reach out and help others, regardless if it's just a smile, an encouraging word, a prayer, or a hug. Amen."

And if anyone gives even a cup of cold water to one of these little ones who is my disciple, truly I tell you, that person will certainly not lose their reward.
Matthew 10:42 NIV

DAY 297
Ridicule

"*Lord,* help me to see that very often people ridicule what they don't understand. As I travel on my spiritual journey, there will probably be times when I get ridiculed. Cause me to understand that the soldiers at the cross ridiculed Jesus, and if people did that to Him, they will probably do that to me. Give me the strength today to be stronger than the insults hurled at me. Amen."

If you are insulted for the name of Christ, you are blessed, because the Spirit of glory and of God rests upon you.
1 Peter 4:14 ESV

DAY 298
Righteous Living

"*Lord*, society tries to teach us that there is no wrong or right way to live. There are no moral absolutes. But the Bible teaches us that when we order our lives after Your Word, then we are living righteously. Give me the courage to stand for righteousness today. Amen."

Woe to those who call evil good, and good evil; who substitute darkness for light and light for darkness; who substitute bitter for sweet and sweet for bitter!
Isaiah 5:20 NASB

DAY 299

Rights

"*Lord,* You have given me a lot of rights in Your Word. You gave me freedom in many areas of my life. Today teach me to be willing to give up some of my rights when they get in the way of loving others. Never let my right to do something or say something interfere with someone else's best interest. Amen."

Therefore, if what I eat causes my brother or sister to fall into sin, I will never eat meat again, so that I will not cause them to fall.
1 Corinthians 8:13 NIV

DAY 300
Risk-Taking

"*Lord*, living by faith sometimes causes me to take some risks in life. There are times when I think I know Your will, but I am not positive. Help me today not to be afraid of taking some risks in life when there is not a lot at stake. If I make a mistake, You will see me through it. Learning to live by faith takes practice. Amen."

He who observes the wind will not sow, and he who regards the clouds will not reap.
Ecclesiastes 11:4 ESV

DAY 301
Role of Parents

"*Lord*, my kids are only under my supervision for a short time of their life. Help me to take advantage of those few years to make a godly impact on them. Cause me to always take my role as a parent seriously. Amen."

These commandments that I give you today are to be on your hearts. Impress them on your children. Talk about them when you sit at home and when you walk along the road, when you lie down and when you get up.
Deuteronomy 6:6-7 NIV

DAY 302

Rudeness

"*Lord*, help me not to make rudeness a habit in my life. It is so easy to let all of the stresses of life bring me down and cause me to start having a bad attitude. Give me the courage today to start fighting rudeness, and replace it with kindness until kindness becomes a habit. It might take some work but with Your Spirit's help, I know I can do this. Amen."

A person finds joy in giving an apt reply - and how good is a timely word!
Proverbs 15:23 NIV

DAY 303

Rumors

"*Lord*, give me the strength to never listen to rumors. If I listen to them, I am as guilty as the one who is spreading them. Today help me to neither spread rumors nor listen to them. Amen."

You shall not spread a false report. You shall not join hands with a wicked man to be a malicious witness.
Exodus 23:1 ESV

DAY 304
Run the Race

"*Lord*, You have given me a race to run. Help me to run it well. Help me find a pace I can keep that's not too fast or too slow. Cause me today to have endurance so that I can keep on doing the things You have called me to do until my race is completed. Help me to see that many victories are won with consistency by doing the same things over and over. Give me the strength to keep on running. Amen."

Therefore, since we are surrounded by so great a cloud of witnesses, let us also lay aside every weight, and sin which clings so closely, and let us run with endurance the race that is set before us.
Hebrews 12:1 ESV

DAY 305
Sabbath

"*Lord*, You have instructed Your people to set aside a sabbath day weekly and to keep it holy. You made us in such a way that we need continual rest for our body, soul, and spirit. Without rest our bodies will eventually wear out and break down. Teach me to set a day aside weekly to rest and rejuvenate. Amen."

Six days you shall work, but on the seventh day you shall rest. In plowing time and in harvest you shall rest.
Exodus 34:21 ESV

DAY 306

Sadness

"*Lord*, in life there are a lot of things that happen to us that make us sad. We must realize that sadness is an emotion, and You are stronger than our emotions. Whenever we are tempted to be sad, cause us to go to You. We ask that You would fill us with Your joy. Today we ask You to be stronger than our emotions. Amen."

Cast your burden upon the Lord and He will sustain you;
He will never allow the righteous to be shaken.
Psalm 55:22 NASB

DAY 307
Salt

"Lord, You have called us to be the salt of the earth. Salt makes things tastier and palatable. Today wherever I go, cause me to leave behind a fragrant, sweet aroma of You. Let something I say or do make all things a little bit better. Amen."

Let your speech always be gracious, seasoned with salt, so that you may know how you ought to answer each person.
Colossians 4:6 ESV

DAY 308
Satisfaction

"*Lord*, cause me to always understand that I was made to live with You. I was created with purpose, and only when I am fulfilling my purpose will I be satisfied. My purpose is to walk with You on a daily basis and simply to take You with me wherever I go. Today help me to walk with You and as a result find satisfaction in my soul. Amen."

For He has satisfied the thirsty soul, and the hungry soul He has filled with what is good.
Psalm 107:9 NASB

DAY 309
Saying "I Love You"

"*Lord*, help me to see how much power I have in my tongue. Today help me to use it wisely. It's amazing how that one little phrase that costs me nothing can change a life. Help me today to tell more people that I love them. Amen."

Gracious words are like a honeycomb, sweetness to the soul and health to the body.
Proverbs 16:24 ESV

DAY 310
Scared

"*Lord*, when I am afraid teach me to run to You. Always cause me to keep in mind that You are bigger and stronger than the things that strike terror in my heart. Cause me to never become a slave to fear. Today I will bring all the things I fear before You, and I will let You help me get through them. Amen."

You shall not be in dread of them, for the LORD your God is in your midst, a great and awesome God.
Deuteronomy 7:21 ESV

DAY 311
Schedules

"Lord, today I need to have wisdom in making my schedule. There are a lot of things I need to fit into it. I need to schedule time with You in prayer and studying the Word. I need to make time for my loved ones, time for work, time to exercise, and time to wind down and relax. Help me today to create a productive schedule. Amen."

Look careful then how you walk, not as unwise but as wise, making the best use of the time, because the days are evil. Therefore do not be foolish, but understand what the will of the Lord is.
Ephesians 5:15-17 ESV

DAY 312
Scoffers

"*Lord*, You warned us in Your Word that in the last days there would be scoffers who would make fun of You and the Bible. Don't let me be discouraged when I meet these people, knowing that You warned us in advance. Today cause me not to be discouraged when I am exposed to scoffers. Amen."

Most importantly, I want to remind you that in the last days scoffers will come, mocking the truth and following their own desires. They will say, "What happened to the promise that Jesus is coming again? From before the times of our ancestors, everything has remained the same since the world was first created."
2 Peter 3:3-4 NLT

DAY 313
Scripture

"Lord, I thank You for the awesome gift of the Bible. Today teach me how to understand it and apply it to my life. Help me with a great study plan so I can take full advantage of all the wisdom that it contains. Amen."

Such things were written in the Scriptures long ago to teach us. And the Scriptures give us hope and encouragement as we wait patiently for God's promises to be fulfilled.
Romans 15:4 NLT

DAY 314

Seasons

"*Lord*, help me as I go through the seasons of life. Give me wisdom to know that just as the earth goes through seasons of change so will my life. As each season comes it will bring with it many opportunities and blessings, as well as many challenges. Cause me today to focus on the blessings and opportunities of the season I am in and not the challenges. Help me to see the beauty of each season. Amen."

For everything there is a season, a time for every activity under heaven. A time to be born and a time to die. A time to plant and a time to harvest. A time to kill and a time to heal. A time to tear down and a time to build up.
Ecclesiastes 3:1-3 NLT

DAY 315
Seed and Harvest

"*Lord*, You have called me to be a seed planter. If I plant seeds, then I give You something to work with, and You will cause the growth. Today help me to plant the seeds of the gospel in people's hearts, seeds of encouragement, seeds of hope, and seeds of wisdom. Cause me to realize the power of a seed. One seed can produce a huge harvest. Many people who have made a mark on society have had someone once plant a seed in their heart. Help me to be a planter of seeds. Amen."

So neither the one who plants nor the one who waters is anything, but only God, who makes things grow.
1 Corinthians 3:7 NIV

DAY 316
Seek First

"*Lord*, You have told me in Your Word to seek first Your kingdom and Your righteousness, and all these things would be added to my life. You are such a gracious God that You allow me to have a lot of interests in my life that I can pursue and enjoy, just as long as I put You and Your kingdom first. Help me today to make sure that I keep my devotion to You as the first priority in my life. Amen."

But seek first His kingdom and His righteousness, and all these things will be added to you.
Matthew 6:33 NASB

DAY 317
Self-Acceptance

"Lord, help me to accept myself as I am. You made me. Please forgive me for complaining or being unhappy about the way I am. Help me to be comfortable in my skin. Amen."

I will give thanks to You, for I am fearfully and wonderfully made; wonderful are Your works, and my soul knows it very well.
Psalm 139:14 NASB

DAY 318
Self-Centered

"Lord, I need Your help in dealing with my self-centered ways. I was born to want life my own way. Today I ask You to give me some opportunities to practice selflessness. Cause me to not make my life all about me. Amen."

Let no one seek his own good, but that of his neighbor.
1 Corinthians 10:24 NASB

DAY 319
Self-Discipline

"Lord, I can never become who I am suppose to be without Your help. Help me to not get discouraged, because being changed into Christ's likeness is a process and a journey. Today give me the power to be self-disciplined with my spiritual life. Help me to be consistently giving myself to the things I need in order to grow spiritually. Amen."

No discipline seems pleasant at the time, but painful. Later on, however, it produces a harvest of righteousness and peace for those who have been trained by it.
Hebrews 12:11 NIV

DAY 320
Self-Worth

"*Lord*, I am Your child. When I think about that, it blows my mind. That is such a hard fact to wrap my mind around. Help me to meditate on the truth that I am a child of the God who created the universe. If that doesn't give me self-worth, then nothing will. Today I want to simply say thank You so much for accepting me into Your family. Amen."

Are not five sparrows sold for two cents? Yet not one of them is forgotten before God. Indeed, the very hairs of your head are all numbered. Do not fear; you are more valuable than many sparrows.
Luke 12:6-7 NASB

DAY 321
Setting Goals

"Lord, help me to set some long-term and short-term goals for my life. Without setting goals, I will lack motivation. Help me to set some goals in regards to my spiritual life, relational life, and my physical life. Help me set goals that are easily obtainable and that have the capability of making my life better.
Amen."

Good planning and hard work lead to prosperity, but hasty shortcuts lead to poverty.
Proverbs 21:5 NLT

DAY 322
Showing Kindness

"*Lord*, today I will meet a lot of people who don't have an opinion about You, because no one has shown them the great love You have for mankind. Lay things on my heart to do for people and to say to people that will show them Your great love and concern for them. Hopefully they will begin to see what a great God You are. Amen."

O taste and see that the Lord is good; how blessed is the man who takes refuge in Him!
Psalm 34:8 NASB

DAY 323
Shyness

"*Lord*, there are times when I need to speak up and be bold. Today help me not to have a spirit of shyness. Give me the strength to speak up for the things of the kingdom. Amen."

The wicked flee though no one pursues, but the righteous are as bold as a lion.
Proverbs 28:1 NIV

DAY 324
Siblings in Christ

"*Lord*, thank You for my siblings. Remind me that everyone who is a Christian is also my brother and sister, for the Word of God teaches us that whoever does Your will is part of our spiritual family. Today help me to get to know my family in Christ better. I have so much to gain by enhancing my relationships with my brothers and sisters in Christ. Amen."

But Jesus answered the one who was telling Him and said, "Who is My mother and who are My brothers?" And stretching out His hand toward His disciples, He said, "Behold My mother and My brothers! For whoever does the will of My Father who is in heaven, he is My brother and sister and mother."
Matthew 12:48-50 NASB

DAY 325
Simplicity

"*Lord*, Your power and love are often seen in the simple things of life. A simple prayer, a simple gesture, or a simple act of kindness can often turn into something great. Very often in the Bible it was the simple things that made the big headlines. People who were forgiven, people who were accepted, people who were recognized, and people who were chosen to be a part of the group were often the ones who went on to do great things in the Bible. It all started with a simple act. God, help me today to not underestimate the power of a simple deed. Amen."

There is a lad here who has five barley loaves and two fish, but what are these for so many people?
John 6:9 NASB

DAY 326

Sin

"*Lord*, please cause me to see sin the way You see sin. Cause me to understand that sin is a package deal. You get maybe 1% of sinful pleasure in the package and 99% of horribly, destructive repercussions, but you have to take the whole package. Help me to trust that anything You identify as sin in the Bible is bad for me in the long run, or You would not have labeled it as sin. Show me any sins that I need to repent of. Amen."

For the wages of sin is death, but the gift of God is eternal life in Christ Jesus our Lord.
Romans 6:23 NKJV

DAY 327
Sincerity

"*Lord*, we live in a world today where people are so busy that they rarely have time to be sincerely concerned for others. When they do reach out, very often it is because they want something from someone. It takes time and sincere focus to be genuinely concerned about others. Today lay someone on my heart that I can reach out to and be sincerely concerned about. Amen."

Now that you have purified yourselves by obeying the truth so that you have sincere love for each other, love one another deeply, from the heart.
1 Peter 1:22 NIV

DAY 328
Single Parents

"*Lord*, help us to always have a heart of sympathy for single parents and their children. It is really tough to raise kids by yourself and still have time to put into your own life. If it is hard for two parents to do the job of raising kids successfully, then for one parent it is a really tough task. Today cause me to keep any single parents I know in my prayers, and remind me of anything I can occasionally do to make their load lighter. Amen."

A father of the fatherless and a judge for the widows, is God in His holy habitation.
Psalm 68:5 NASB

DAY 329
Soldiers

"*Lord*, there are places in the Bible where we are told to have the mentality of a soldier. There are times when this world feels like a war zone. A soldier has commanders over him, he has weapons that have been given to him to fight with, and he fights so others might experience freedom. Sometimes he has to give up some of his rights for the sake of the calling. Today help me to keep all this in mind as I go throughout my day trying to be a soldier of Jesus Christ. Amen."

Suffer hardship with me, as a good soldier of Christ Jesus.
2 Timothy 2:3 NASB

DAY 330
Spiritual Gifts

"*Lord*, I was put on this earth to do a special job that no one else can do but me. In Your Word we are told that You have given each of us a special gift to help us complete that job. Please help me today to discover my gift and my calling. Amen."

Now about the gifts of the Spirit, brothers and sisters, I do not want you to be uninformed.
1 Corinthians 12:1 NIV

DAY 331
Spiritual Growth

"*Lord*, You have called me to grow spiritually. Much in the same way as I grew physically, I am to grow spiritually. Help me to continue growing in the spirit until I leave this earth. Today help me to stay dedicated to growing in love, grace, wisdom, knowledge, and influence. Amen."

But grow in the grace and knowledge of our Lord and Savior Jesus Christ.
2 Peter 3:18 NASB

DAY 332
Staying Healthy

"*Lord*, help me to take good care of my body, knowing that my body is essential to carrying out my purpose on this earth. Don't let me wait until I am diagnosed with an illness to change my health habits. Today motivate me to make it a priority in my life to be healthy. Amen."

Or do you not know that your body is a temple of the Holy Spirit who is in you, whom you have from God, and that you are not your own? For you have been bought with a price: therefore glorify God in your body.
1 Corinthians 6:19-20 NASB

DAY 333
Steadfast

"*Lord*, not much good in life comes to us without some amount of steadfastness. Give me the discipline to finish everything that I feel led to start. Don't let me become a habitual quitter in life - someone who starts a lot of things, but rarely sees things through to completion. God, help me to count the cost before I commit to things, so I can become a steadfast person. Amen."

Therefore, my dear brothers and sisters, stand firm. Let nothing move you. Always give yourselves fully to the work of the Lord, because you know that your labor in the Lord is not in vain.
1 Corinthians 15:58 NIV

DAY 334
Stewardship

"*Lord*, You are constantly giving me things to give to others. I am called to be a steward of those things. Today help me to understand that as You bless me and encourage me, I am to turn around and bless and encourage others. You give me things to pass along. I am not on this earth to be a spiritual hoarder, but I am called to be a giver. Amen."

Each of you should use whatever gift you have received to serve others, as faithful stewards of God's grace in its various forms.
1 Peter 4:10 NIV

DAY 335
Stillness

"*Lord*, cause me to not always think I have to be doing something, saying something, or listening to something. Free me from being addicted to my cell phone. Help me to discipline myself to a daily time of stillness, so I can hear Your voice and collect my thoughts. Amen."

He says, "Be still, and know that I am God ..."
Psalm 46:10 NIV

DAY 336

Stress

"*Lord*, give me the power and the wisdom to not let stress rule my life. Cause me to take everything that causes stress in my life to You in prayer. Give me the constant understanding that worrying about things will not change anything. Give me the discipline today to set a designated time aside to work on my problems. After I have done all I can do, give me the power to set my problems aside and refuse to think about them for the rest of my day. Amen."

Can any one of you by worrying add a single hour to your life?
Matthew 6:27 NIV

DAY 337
Studying the Bible

"Lord, give me the discipline to set aside a time every day to study Your Word. Help me to discover the deep riches of knowledge and wisdom that are hidden in the pages of the Bible. Today cause Your Spirit to help me to see life-changing principles as I study Your Word. Amen."

And you will know the truth, and the truth will set you free.
John 8:32 NLT

DAY 338
Submission

"*Lord*, help me to see that You have called me to submit myself to others whom You have put in my life as spiritual, authoritative figures. Cause me to not do this with a rebellious heart but a willing and pleasant spirit, knowing that this is pleasing to You. Amen."

In the same way, you who are younger, submit yourselves to your elders. All of you, clothe yourselves with humility toward one another, because, "God opposes the proud but shows favor to the humble."
1 Peter 5:5 NIV

DAY 339
Teachable

"*Lord*, cause me to always keep a teachable heart. Don't let me ever think that I know more than I do. Today help me to ask a lot of questions from those older and wiser than myself. Amen."

Let the wise listen and add to their learning, and let the discerning get guidance.
Proverbs 1:5 NIV

DAY 340
Television

"*Lord*, help me to control my TV habits. Cause me to use television wisely. Let it be a tool to help me relax, and not become something I get addicted to and can't live without. Help me to see the value of occasional quiet time in the home, and convict me of spending too much time with my television set. Give me wisdom and insight into other things I can do nightly in place of always watching television. Amen."

Turn away my eyes from looking at worthless things, and revive me in Your way.
Psalm 119:37 NKJV

DAY 341
Temptation

"*Lord*, help me today to beat my temptations. Keep reminding me that temptation is not a sin, only yielding to it is. Don't let me feel condemned for being tempted. Today show me what righteous things I need to put in place of the wrong things that are tempting me. Amen."

Keep watching and praying that you may not enter into temptation; the spirit is willing, but the flesh is weak.
Matthew 26:41 NASB

DAY 342

Testimonies

"*Lord*, help me to understand the power of testimonies. When I share with people the stories of how You made a way for me when there seemed to be no way, it gets people's attention. It takes tests in order to have testimonies. Today let me see each test, trial, and temptation as an opportunity for a testimony. Amen."

This confirms that what I told you about Christ is true.
1 Corinthians 1:6 NLT

DAY 343
Thank You

"*Lord*, don't let me underestimate the power of a simple thank you. Today help me to start saying thank you to people that You lay on my heart. Let me say thanks to my friends for being there when I needed them. Let me also say thank you to my parents, my siblings, my boss, my pastor, my doctor, and anyone else I can think of. Amen."

I have not stopped thanking God for you.
I pray for you constantly.
Ephesians 1:16 NLT

DAY 344
The Afterlife

"*Lord*, today let me think about my loved ones in heaven. Cause me to know that someday I will be joining them. Today I thank You that I will live forever. Amen."

For to me, to live is Christ and to die is gain.
Philippians 1:21 NASB

DAY 345
The Armor of God

"Lord, the Bible teaches me about the armor of God. Without it I will not be able to stand against my spiritual enemy. Today cause me to protect myself from the lies of the enemy by equipping myself with the truth of Your Word. Today give me a verse to combat anything that is stressing me out. Amen."

He put on righteousness like a breastplate, and a helmet of salvation on His head; and He put on garments of vengeance for clothing and wrapped Himself with zeal as a mantle.
Isaiah 59:17 NASB

DAY 346

The Family

"*Lord*, help me today to enlarge my family. Cause me to see that I have brothers and sisters in the family of God who may not be part of my biological family but are part of my spiritual family. Show me ways to enhance my relationship with them. Help me to start treating them like family, and help me to see my responsibility toward them. Amen."

But those who won't care for their relatives, especially those in their own household, have denied the true faith. Such people are worse than unbelievers.
1 Timothy 5:8 NLT

DAY 347
The Flesh

"Lord, show me today the difference between the flesh and the spirit. You have told us that the flesh sets its desires against the things of the spirit. Today there is a war going on between my flesh and my spirit, so teach me how to win this war. Let me begin by feeding the spirit more than I feed the flesh and denying the flesh and its desires. Today give me the strength I need to say no to the flesh and yes to the spirit. Amen."

For those who are according to the flesh set their minds on the things of the flesh, but those who are according to the Spirit, the things of the Spirit.
Romans 8:5 NASB

DAY 348
Thoughts

"*Lord*, cause me to see that what I allow my mind to focus on has the potential to influence the way my life turns out. My mind affects my emotions, my emotions affect my actions, and my actions if repeated over and over will result in a lifestyle. Today cause me to be cognizant of what I allow my mind to focus on. Amen."

Watch over your heart with all diligence, for from it flow the springs of life.
Proverbs 4:23 NASB

DAY 349

Time

"*Lord*, help me to use my time wisely. Today show me anything in my life that is a waste of time and not benefiting me or the kingdom of God in any way. Give me the wisdom I need to divide my time between You, my career, my family, rest, and recreation. Amen."

Redeeming the time, because the days are evil.
Ephesians 5:16 NKJV

DAY 350
Timing

"*Lord*, sometimes I get very impatient waiting on You to act in my life. Please forgive me for my spirit of impatience. Let me never forget that Your timing is perfect. You know when I am ready for my prayers to be answered, and You know when circumstances are right for me to have doors of opportunity opened. Help me today not to grow impatient. Amen."

This vision is for a future time. It describes the end, and it will be fulfilled. If it seems slow in coming, wait patiently, for it will surely take place. It will not be delayed.
Habakkuk 2:3 NLT

DAY 351
Tired

"Lord, I sometimes get very tired and want to quit. I sometimes want to quit trying in my relationships, trying at my place of employment, trying to keep my body in shape, or trying in my walk with You. I get discouraged and want to give up. Today please reinvigorate me with new strength and a spirit of endurance. Amen."

> *For I satisfy the weary ones and refresh everyone who languishes.*
> *Jeremiah 31:25 NASB*

DAY 352
Tolerance

"Lord, help me to know that tolerance is not the same as acceptance. There will always be people on this earth that live and act in ways that I do not approve of, but they have a right to live their life the way that they choose as long as it does not interfere with my life. Today help me to be tolerant of these people and agree to disagree with their behavior. Amen."

So in everything, do to others what you would have them do to you, for this sums up the Law and the Prophets.
Matthew 7:12 NIV

DAY 353
Tomorrow

"Lord, don't let me always be anxious for tomorrow while life passes me by today. Don't let me put off things for tomorrow that I can do today. It is important that I live with my eyes open and keep my attention on the present, or many opportunities will pass me by. Amen."

Do not boast about tomorrow, for you do not know what a day may bring.
Proverbs 27:1 NIV

DAY 354
Tough Love

"Lord, help me to not confuse true love with being a people pleaser. There will be times when I will have to make decisions regarding those I love based upon their best interests. I might have to lovingly give a rebuke or refuse to do something their way. If it's a child, I may have to discipline them. All of these things I am called to do because I love them. Give me the courage to express tough love when necessary. Amen."

Am I now trying to win the approval of human beings, or of God? Or am I trying to please people? If I were still trying to please people, I would not be a servant of Christ.
Galatians 1:10 NIV

DAY 355
Tough Times

"*Lord*, everyone has to go through tough times. It's part of life, and it is also how we grow. No one can avoid tough times. Give me the discipline to equip myself today with a good support team, a healthy daily regiment of the Word and prayer, as well as a good mentor in my life, so that I will be prepared when the tough times come. Amen."

Be strong and courageous, do not be afraid or tremble at them, for the LORD your God is the one who goes with you. He will not fail you or forsake you.
Deuteronomy 31:6 NASB

DAY 356
Transformation

"*Lord*, Your will for me is spiritual transformation. The world wants to conform me to their way of life, but You have called me to be in constant change as the character of Christ is developed in me. My spiritual growth should be constant and consistent. Today help me to embrace the things in life that cause my character to grow deeper no matter how uncomfortable they may be. Amen."

But we all, with unveiled face, beholding as in a mirror the glory of the Lord, are being transformed into the same image from glory to glory, just as from the Lord, the Spirit.
2 Corinthians 3:18 NASB

DAY 357
Unconditional Love

"Lord, I thank You so much for Your unconditional love. That simply means that because I have accepted You into my life, there is nothing I can do to make You stop loving me. Today, knowing that love is a commitment of the will and not just a feeling, give me the strength to love others with Your unconditional love. Amen."

Can anything ever separate us from Christ's love? Does it mean he no longer loves us if we have trouble or calamity, or are persecuted, or hungry, or destitute, or in danger, or threatened with death?
Romans 8:35 NLT

DAY 358
Unforgiveness

"Lord, because You have forgiven me time after time, oftentimes for the same sin, I must do the same for others. A spirit of unforgiveness is not acceptable in Your sight. Today show me anyone that I haven't forgiven, and then give me the strength to forgive them and let them go free of their wrongdoing. Amen."

And forgive us our debts, as we also have forgiven our debtors.
Matthew 6:12 NASB

DAY 359
Ungratefulness

"*Lord*, thank You for everything You have given me and every blessing You have bestowed on me. Don't let me ever take Your loving grace for granted. Today I just want to say thank You. Amen."

Because, although they knew God, they did not glorify Him as God, nor were thankful, but became futile in their thoughts, and their foolish hearts were darkened.
Romans 1:21 NKJV

DAY 360
Uniqueness

"*Lord*, I thank You that I am fearfully and wonderfully made. There is no other person on this planet just like me. Please help me to use my uniqueness in such a way that You will receive glory through me. Amen."

Thank you for making me so wonderfully complex! Your workmanship is marvelous - how well I know it.
Psalm 139:14 NLT

DAY 361
Values

"*Lord*, You have created me to be holy and separated from the world. You have also called me to live a righteous life. You want me to value the things that You value. Today cause me to make sure that I have a clear-cut set of values in my life that will help me accomplish those goals. Amen."

Whoever walks in integrity walks securely, but whoever takes crooked paths will be found out.
Proverbs 10:9 NIV

DAY 362

Vengeance

"Lord, help me to believe that You will deal with those who have hurt me. The Bible says that I am the apple of Your eye. Please forgive me for all those times I have tried to avenge myself. In the future, help me to resist that temptation and to let You handle that for me. Amen."

Never take your own revenge, beloved, but leave room for the wrath of God, for it is written, "Vengeance is Mine, I will repay," says the Lord.
Romans 12:19 NASB

DAY 363
Vessels

"*Lord*, help me to be a vessel of Your love and power. Like an electrical current travels through a wire, let me be a human vessel through which Your Spirit can flow. Amen."

Therefore if anyone cleanses himself from the latter, he will be a vessel for honor, sanctified and useful for the Master, prepared for every good work.
2 Timothy 2:21 NKJV

DAY 364

Virtue

"*Lord*, someone said that a virtue is the quality that lies between two extremes. Please help me to be a virtuous person in all areas of life. Cause me not to be angry about small, petty things but to have righteous indignation. Help me to be loving but not enabling, and help me to be holy but not legalistic. Amen."

Now for this very reason also, applying all diligence, in your faith supply moral excellence, and in your moral excellence, knowledge.
2 Peter 1:5 NASB

DAY 365
Warriors

"*Lord*, help me today to be a warrior for You. Cause me to see myself as someone who is called to fight for godliness and righteousness in a world that is fighting against those very things. Today give me the spirit of a warrior and make me strong. Amen."

A time to love and a time to hate. A time for war and a time for peace.
Ecclesiastes 3:8 NLT

ABOUT THE AUTHOR

Ron Vietti is currently the Lead Pastor at Valley Bible Fellowship, the church he and his wife, Debbie, pioneered in Bakersfield, California in 1971. He is the author of *Tribal Influence, Polyester People, Conspiracy of Silence,* along with three children's books: *Oreo Finds a Friend, Bella Goes to School,* and *Charlie Finds a Home.*

Ron is a sports enthusiast. Whether it's NFL, NCAA, NBA, MLB, or UFC, you can find him fully engaged. He also enjoys spending time with the love of his life of 50 years, Debbie, as well as his kids and grandkids.

CONNECT WITH THE AUTHOR

BLOG: ronvietti.com
FACEBOOK: /pastorronvietti
INSTAGRAM: @ronvietti
TWITTER: @ronvietti

AUTHOR'S CORNER

Check out additional resources by Ron Vietti.

Tribal Influence is a conversation starter as we become connected to different types of people and break down some human barriers and prejudices that have plagued humanity for decades. It brings to light the purpose of restoring broken relationships and being connected to others in a meaningful way.

Polyester People is for those who are tired of religion and are brave enough to go back and reexamine the scriptures to see what they really say. Not for the spiritually content, this book is about becoming the people that God wants us to be so that we can reach the world around us.

Conspiracy of Silence is about finding balance in developing a walk with God similar to the kind of relationship that the Old and New Testament saints had with God. Without this kind of walk, the church will most definitely continue living in defeat. Satan has always been committed to his conspiracy of silencing the voice of God in our lives.

AUTHOR'S CORNER

Adventures of the Simple Life Ranch is a three-book children's series written by Ron Vietti that serves as a guide for parents and teachers to reinforce a stronger value system in each child's life. Each book contains activities and curriculum as additional resources.

Adventures of the Simple Life Ranch contains the following books:

Oreo Finds a Friend serves to teach us about bullying, and how individual kids can befriend those that others don't treat well.

Bella Goes to School serves to teach and encourage children to see the value of developing relationships with other children. We all have something to share and learn from one another.

Charlie Finds a Home serves to teach children the need to care about those who are not as fortunate as others. We all need to be kind and care for those around us.

INDEX

Abandonment	1
Absentminded	2
Acceptance	3
Accomplishment	4
Accusations	5
Addiction	6
Advice	7
Affirmation	8
Ambition	9
Angels	10
Anger	11
Answers	12
Apology	13
Appreciation	14
Arrogance	15
Assumption	16
Assurance	17
Availability	18
Awe	19
Backsliding	20
Balance	21
Bashful	22
Basics	23
Beginning	24
Behavior	25
Bible	26
Bitterness	27
Blame	28
Blessing	29
Body	30
Brevity	31
Burnout	32
Caring	33
Carnality	34
Celebrate	35
Challenges	36
Change	37
Character	38
Charity	39
Cheerful	40
Choices	41
Commitment	42
Communication	43
Community	44
Comparing	45
Compassion	46
Competence	47
Compensation	48
Competition	49
Complaining	50
Compromise	51
Condemnation	52
Confession	53
Confidence	54
Confidentiality	55
Conflict	56

INDEX

Confusion	57
Conscience	58
Consequences	59
Consistency	60
Contentment	61
Control	62
Convenience	63
Conversation	64
Conviction	65
Correction	66
Culture	67
Death	68
Debt	69
Decisions	70
Dedication	71
Deeds	72
Defeat	73
Denial	74
Depression	75
Design	76
Desire	77
Despair	78
Destiny	79
Determination	80
Devil	81
Difference	82
Disagreement	83
Disbelief	84
Discernment	85
Discipline	86
Discrimination	87
Dishonesty	88
Disobedience	89
Disrespect	90
Distractions	91
Doors	92
Dreams	93
Easter	94
Elderly	95
Embarrassment	96
Embracing	97
Emotion	98
Empathy	99
Empty	100
Encouragement	101
Endurance	102
Enemies	103
Energy	104
Enjoyment	105
Enthusiasm	106
Eternity	107
Ethics	108
Evangelizing	109
Exaggeration	110
Example	111
Exercise	112

INDEX

Excess	113	Gratification	141
Excuses	114	Greatness	142
Failure	115	Greed	143
Faith	116	Grief	144
Family	117	Growth	145
Fear	118	Grudges	146
Feelings	119	Grumbling	147
Fellowship	120	Guidance	148
Fidelity	121	Guilt	149
Finances	122	Habits	150
First Love	123	Happiness	151
Fitness	124	Hard Work	152
Flesh	125	Hatred	153
Food	126	Healing	154
Forgetting	127	Hearing God	155
Forgiveness	128	Heaven	156
Forsaken	129	Heresy	157
Freedom	130	Hoarding	158
Friends	131	Hobbies	159
Fruitfulness	132	Holiness	160
Funerals	133	Honesty	161
Future	134	Honor	162
Giving	135	Honoring God	163
Gloating	136	Hope	164
Goals	137	Hospitality	165
Gossip	138	Houses	166
Government	139	Humanity	167
Grace	140	Humility	168

INDEX

Humor	169	Justification	197
Hunger	170	Kids	198
Hypocrisy	171	Kindness	199
Identity	172	Laziness	200
Idleness	173	Learning	201
Idolatry	174	Lessons	202
Ignorance	175	Listening	203
Illness	176	Loneliness	204
Immorality	177	Longevity	205
Immortality	178	Losing	206
Impatience	179	Love	207
Imperfection	180	Lowly	208
Impossibility	181	Lukewarm	209
Increase	182	Lust	210
Independence	183	Lying	211
Inheritance	184	Manners	212
Insecurity	185	Marriage	213
Inspiration	186	Materialism	214
Instruction	187	Maturity	215
Integrity	188	Mean People	216
Intimidation	189	Meditation	217
Intoxication	190	Meekness	218
Investing	191	Memories	219
Irresponsibility	192	Miracles	220
Irritable	193	Missions	221
Jealousy	194	Mistakes	222
Journey	195	Modesty	223
Judgmentalism	196	Money	224

INDEX

Moral Absolutes	225
Morality	226
Mothers	227
Mourning	228
Mouth	229
Moving On	230
Music	231
Needs	232
Neighbor	233
Not Defeated	234
Obedience	235
Old Age	236
Opinions	237
Optimism	238
Organization	239
Our Past	240
Our Weakness	241
Overcoming	242
Pain	243
Parables	244
Parents	245
Parental Discipline	246
Partiality	247
Peace	248
People in Heaven	249
Perseverance	250
Plans	251
Pleasure	252
Popularity	253
Potential	254
Poverty	255
Power of Prayer	256
Power of Testimony	257
Power of God	258
Praying for Others	259
Predestination	260
Prejudice	261
Presence of God	262
Priorities	263
Protection	264
Provision	265
Questions	266
Quitting	267
Racism	268
Raising Children	269
Reading God's Word	270
Real Love	271
Reap What You Sow	272
Reasons	273
Reconciliation	274
Recreation	275
Reflection	276
Regrets	277
Regular Church Attendance	278
Rejection	279
Rejoicing	280

INDEX

Relationships	281	Saying "I Love You"	309
Relaxation	282	Scared	310
Relevance	283	Schedules	311
Reliability	284	Scoffers	312
Remembrance	285	Scripture	313
Renewing the Mind	286	Seasons	314
Repentance	287	Seed and Harvest	315
Reputation	288	Seek First	316
Resentment	289	Self-Acceptance	317
Resolving Conflict	290	Self-Centered	318
Restoring Friendships	291	Self-Discipline	319
Resurrection of Christ	292	Self-Worth	320
Revealing Secrets	293	Setting Goals	321
Revenge	294	Showing Kindness	322
Reverence	295	Shyness	323
Rewards in Heaven	296	Siblings in Christ	324
Ridicule	297	Simplicity	325
Righteous Living	298	Sin	326
Rights	299	Sincerity	327
Risk-Taking	300	Single Parents	328
Role of Parents	301	Soldiers	329
Rudeness	302	Spiritual Gifts	330
Rumors	303	Spiritual Growth	331
Run the Race	304	Staying Healthy	332
Sabbath	305	Steadfast	333
Sadness	306	Stewardship	334
Salt	307	Stillness	335
Satisfaction	308	Stress	336

INDEX

Studying the Bible	337
Submission	338
Teachable	339
Television	340
Temptation	341
Testimonies	342
Thank You	343
The Afterlife	344
The Armor of God	345
The Family	346
The Flesh	347
Thoughts	348
Time	349
Timing	350
Tired	351
Tolerance	352
Tomorrow	353
Tough Love	354
Tough Times	355
Transformation	356
Unconditional Love	357
Unforgiveness	358
Ungratefulness	359
Uniqueness	360
Values	361
Vengeance	362
Vessels	363
Virtue	364
Warriors	365